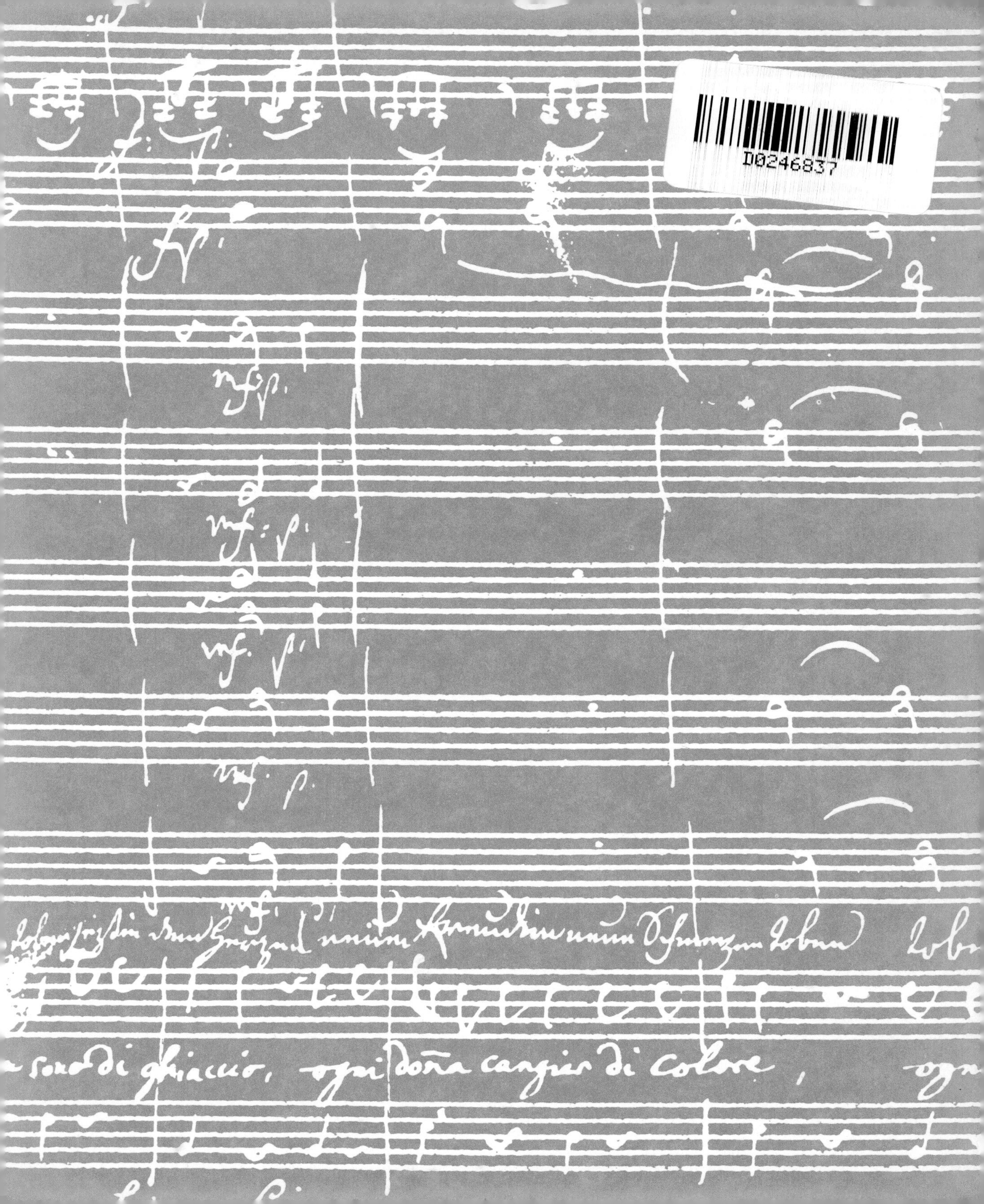

D0246837

Classical Music
A New Way of
Listening

Alexander Waugh

De Agostini *Editions*

CONTENTS

CD RUNNING ORDER

1 Mozart: Symphony No. 40 in G minor, K. 550. First movement (extract)

2 Chopin: Waltz in E flat, op. 18 (extract)

3 Chopin: Waltz in A flat, op. 42 (extract)

4 Chopin: Waltz in A minor, op. 34, No. 2 (extract)

5 Wagner: *Tristan and Isolde*. Prelude, Act 1 (extract)

6 Schubert: *Winterreise*, D. 911. "Gute Nacht" (extracts)

7 Mozart: *Don Giovanni*. Act 1 recitative, "Ma qual mai s'offre"

8 Beethoven: Piano Sonata No. 8 in C minor, op. 13 ("Pathétique"). First movement (extract)

9 Offenbach: *The Tales of Hoffmann*. Act IV, "Belle nuit, ô nuit d'amour" (Barcarolle, extract)

10 Debussy: *Rêverie* (extract)

11 Gilbert and Sullivan: *The Mikado*. Act 1 trio, "I am so proud"

12 Mendelssohn: String Quartet No. 6 in F minor, op. 80. First movement (extract)

13 Brahms: Symphony No. 3 in F major, op. 90. Third movement (extract)

14 Debussy: "Clair de lune" (extract)

15 Fauré: *Pavane*, op. 50 (extract)

16 Handel: *Messiah*. Part 1, "Thus saith the Lord" (extract)

17 Vivaldi: *The Four Seasons*, "Autumn." Third movement (extract)

18 Beethoven: Symphony No. 8 in F major, op. 93. First movement (extract)

19 Beethoven: Symphony No. 5 in C minor, op. 67. Third movement (extract)

20 Liszt: Transcendental Study No. 2 in A minor (extract)

21 Beethoven: String Quartet No. 15 in A minor, op. 132. Final movement (extract)

22 Beethoven: Piano Sonata No. 8 in C minor, op. 13 ("Pathétique"). Second movement (extract)

23 Beethoven: Symphony No. 1 in C major, op. 21. Fourth movement (extract)

24 Beethoven: Piano Concerto No. 5 in E flat major, op. 73 ("Emperor"). Third movement (extract)

25 Beethoven: String Quartet No. 7 in F major, op. 59, No. 1 ("Rasumovsky"). First movement (extract)

26 Beethoven: Piano Sonata No. 32 in C minor, op. 111. First movement (extract)

27 Beethoven: String Quartet No. 13 in B flat major, op. 130. Fifth movement ("Cavatina," extract)

28 Tchaikovsky: *1812 Overture*, op. 49

29 Tallis: *Audivi vocem*

30 Vivaldi: *The Four Seasons*, "Winter." First movement

31 Mozart: *The Marriage of Figaro*. Act 1 aria, "Non so più cosa son"

32 Beethoven: Piano Sonata No. 8 in C minor, op. 13 ("Pathétique"). Third movement

33 Schubert: Piano Quintet in A major, D. 667 ("The Trout"). Fourth movement: Variations

34 Debussy: *La Mer*. Second movement, "Jeux de vagues"

35 Dvořák: Bagatelle, op. 47, No. 1

36 Liszt: Transcendental Study No. 1 in C major

37 Purcell: *Funeral Music for Queen Mary*. March

38 Verdi: *Il trovatore*. Act III recitative, "L'onda de'suoni"

INTRODUCTION

Wanting to appreciate classical music and actually having the confidence to appreciate it are, unfortunately, two different things. Everyone knows that classical music at its best is capable of moving listeners to tears, absorbing their complete attention, even changing their lives. But what is music "at its best?" How can listeners be moved to tears by what is essentially just a noise? And what exactly is it that so avidly consumes their concentration? *Classical Music: A New Way of Listening* is a beginner's guide that suggests an easy new approach to the art of listening, helping you to focus on music's emotional message rather than on its technicalities. For those who are daunted by the names and shapes of musical instruments, or the words and terms of musical conversation, simple sections covering these issues have been specially included, but, for the main part, this is a book about how to respond to the sound of music, choose which pieces to listen to and discover and develop your own musical tastes. If classical music has not changed your life already, *Classical Music: A New Way of Listening* will help to change it for you now.

Chapter 1
What Is This Thing Called Music?

My idea is that there is music in the air, music all around us, the world is full of it and you simply take as much as you require.
Edward Elgar (1857–1934)

It is scarcely possible to imagine a world where music doesn't exist. Even without a radio or a CD player at home, we are constantly exposed to music on the television, at the cinema, in shops and lifts, and even on the telephone. Elgar implies that music is a human requirement, just like the air we breathe or the food we eat: without it perhaps we might die, or at least go mad.

Classical music has been a booming industry on a global scale since the early 1980s. Sales of classical music are higher than ever before, and more live concerts are performed around the world with each year that passes. Perhaps this is all attributable to the clean digital sound of the compact disc, or CD, a medium particularly suited to the textures and patterns of classical music. Or is it something else, something deeper that is driving so many new listeners toward the classics? Many people are drawn in because they believe classical music offers them a form of spiritual fulfilment. It is, after all, powerful, beautiful, moving and elusive in a way that other music is not, and it appears to express things that cannot be translated into the words of everyday language. Classical music provides, in the same way as religion, a basic mystery and, as Albert Einstein put it, "the most beautiful experience we can have is the mysterious."

What Is Classical Music?

I hate quotations.

Ralph Waldo Emerson in his journal, May 1849

Music is an extraordinarily difficult concept to describe in words. Literally hundreds of definitions of music have been penned over the centuries, many of which seem to go round and round in circles, but a few are genuinely thought-provoking. Some marvel at the heavenly beauty of music while others attempt to reduce the art form to a pat scientific formula. There follows a short selection of notable definitions, but for those who share Ralph Waldo Emerson's marked dislike for quotations, skip on, skip on!

Music is the eye of the ear.
   Thomas Draxe (d. 1618)

Music is nothing else but wild sounds civilised into time and tune.
   Thomas Fuller (1608–61)

Music is a secret and unconscious mathematical problem of the soul.
   Gottfried Wilhelm Leibniz (1646–1716)

Music is the only sensual pleasure without vice.
   Dr. Samuel Johnson (1709–84)

Music is said to be the speech of angels: in fact, nothing among the utterances allowed to man is felt to be so divine. It brings us near to the infinite.
   Thomas Carlyle (1795–1881)

Music is a strange thing. I would almost say it is a miracle. For it stands halfway between thought and phenomenon, between spirit and matter, a sort of nebulous mediator, like and unlike each of the things it mediates – spirit that requires manifestation in time, and matter that can do without space.
   Heinrich Heine (1797–1856)

Music is the only noise for which one is obliged to pay.
   Alexandre Dumas (1802–70)

Music is the universal language of mankind.
   Henry Wadsworth Longfellow (1807–82)

Music is itself.
   Eduard Hanslick (1825–1904)

Music is the art of thinking with sounds.
   Jules Combarieu (1859–1916)

Music is the arithmetic of sounds as optics is the geometry of light.
   Claude Debussy (1862–1918)

Music is the best means we have of digesting time.
   W.H. Auden (1907–73)

Music might be defined as a system of proportions in the service of a spiritual impulse.
   George Crumb (b. 1929)

Angels Playing Musical Instruments by Francesco Botticini, c.1475–97.

11

It would be virtually impossible to come up with a definition that pleased everyone, because listening is a highly subjective experience. It is so subjective, in fact, that there is no such thing as a right or wrong emotional response to any piece of music. Even "experts" disagree with one another. Take the famous opening of Mozart's Symphony No. 40 in G minor, featured on **Track 1** of the accompanying CD. Does it, broadly speaking, make you feel happy or sad? Or, to put it another way, how do you think the composer was feeling when he wrote it? Charles Rosen, one of the world's most respected scholars of Mozart's music and the Classical period, believes this piece to be one of his "supreme expressions of suffering and terror," whereas Alfred Einstein, one of America's leading musicologists (and cousin of the great physicist, Albert), compares the same piece with Voltaire's *Candide* – a novel famous for its irony, satire and whimsical wit. "Between *Candide* and the G minor Symphony," Einstein wrote in his biography of Mozart, "there is a real kinship." He goes on to quote another source that describes the same music as a model of "Grecian lightness and grace."

Of course, neither scholar can be wrong, however strongly their views conflict, because reactions to music are so personal. Beauty, after all, is in the eye – or the ear – of the beholder, so there's absolutely no

Ideals of beauty are as subjective in art as in music, as shown by these two very different representations of female beauty. *Left* Detail from Botticelli's *The Birth of Venus*, c.1485. *Right* Tamara de Lempicka, *Young Girl in Green*, 1927.

need to be embarrassed about your musical tastes. There is no such thing as a hierarchy of musical greatness – and claims to the contrary are pure snobbery. Works such as Vivaldi's *The Four Seasons* or Albinoni's *Adagio* are popular because they are enduring masterpieces, and there is no less value in appreciating these than there is in appreciating any other piece of classical music.

Cultural Insecurity and Musical Snobbery

I only know two tunes; one of them is "Yankee Doodle" and the other isn't.
Ulysses S. Grant (1822–85), U.S. President

Classical music snobbery isn't new: it's been with us for millennia. Even Plato, who perhaps should have known better, was guilty of muddle-headedness on the subject. He seemed to believe that only the elite could appreciate music:

The excellence of music is to be measured by pleasure. But the pleasure must not be that of chance persons; the fairest music is that which delights the best and best educated, and especially that which delights the one man who is pre-eminent in virtue and education. (Laws)

Another misconception about classical music was that only certain cultures could enjoy it. In 1907, for example, a Japanese man named Jihei Hashigushi wrote a letter to a New York newspaper after the American premiere of Puccini's opera *Madame Butterfly* (a performance in which the greatest tenor of the time, Enrico Caruso, was singing the part of the hero Mario Cavaradossi), expressing the opinion that being Japanese somehow prohibited him from enjoying western classical music. "I can say nothing for the music of Madama Butterfly," he lamented. "Western music is too complicated for a Japanese. Even Caruso's celebrated singing does not appeal very much more than the barking of a dog in faraway woods."

If Mr. Hashigushi had lived to see the popularity of western classical music in Japan today, he might have had to swallow his words. Not only is Japan now the second-largest market for classical CDs (the U.S. being the largest), but many Japanese musicians rank among the world's greatest classical performers; and classical concerts in Tokyo, unlike elsewhere in the world, are always sold out.

Confucius (551–479 BC) provides us with one of the earliest examples of musical bigotry. In his view, only the most virtuous in society were fit to enjoy music: "If a man be without the virtues proper to humanity, what has he to do with music?"

Listening to classical music doesn't require huge intellectual effort or vast musical know-how. As you develop a love for music you will inevitably learn more about it, but you don't have to be a music scholar to enjoy it. In some cases the reverse can be true. When you discover, for example, that the first movement of nearly every piece by Mozart features a note-by-note repetition of the first half, will you enjoy it more? Or is it possible that this information will rob the music of some of its freshness and mystery, and that the return of a beautiful melody will suddenly sound less magically inspired? There is no evidence that being able to read music or play a musical instrument will sharpen your emotional responses to a piece of music. In fact, those who follow concerts with printed copies of the music glued to their eyes are generally too preoccupied to be able to enjoy the music properly and usually end up missing the fun. So don't let anyone tell you that only experts can properly appreciate a great piece of music.

Sadly, musical narrow-mindedness hasn't quite disappeared and – ironically – lovers of popular music are often just as guilty of snobbery as classical fans:

The trumpeter Wynton Marsalis plays as much jazz as classical music, and is a key figure in the battle to rid classical music of its snobbish image.

THE CLASSICAL BUFF	THE POP BUFF
"Why does pop have to have such a dominant and intrusive rhythm section and why is the beat always so inflexible?"	"Why does classical music keep changing moods and spoiling itself with boring parts?"
"If only pop did not need to be so loud all the time."	"If only I didn't have to keep turning the volume up and down."
"It's too simplistic."	"It's too complicated."
"It's irritating, boring and rigid."	"It's rigid, boring and irritating."

In fact, classical music and pop music have many features in common, and there's no reason why you shouldn't be able to enjoy both. The secret is to listen to each in a slightly different way. Pop songs generally have a steady beat, a fairly constant volume, a relatively simple pattern of chords and melodies, and, most importantly, lyrics that tell us what the music is about. In classical music, on the other hand, the rhythm keeps changing, and so does the

There are no barriers to this universal art. From left to right: José Carreras, Placido Domingo and Luciano Pavarotti, who achieved pop-star status following the worldwide success of their "Three Tenors Concert" in Rome on July 7, 1990

key, and a huge array of instruments is used to create changing themes, with the volume always rising and falling. Classical music often has no words, so you have to listen to the "vocabulary" it uses: rhythm, instrumentation, and so on, and to see how these produce changes in mood and other musical developments. We will look in detail at how to listen in Chapter 3, but the point here is that there's no need to feel intimidated by classical music or classical music experts.

Is Classical Music Really Emotional?

Music was invented to deceive and delude mankind.

Ephorus (*c*.405–330 BC), from his preface to *Historiai*

Tragedy makes us sad, and good fortune makes us happy. Almost every day of our lives we are subjected to the lesser emotions of frustration, anger, relief, disappointment, excitement and anticipation, as well as thousands of other emotional ripples triggered by the events of our lives. Even if these turn out to be unimportant in the long run, they are real enough at the time; we can easily identify them and understand the reasons we have felt them. We know, too, that great music, like the events of our lives, has the power to move us – but why? Why should music, which is really no more than a sequence of organized sounds, be able to affect our emotions in any way? Is there any logical reason why a series of abstract noises, heard from the comfort of an armchair,

should possibly cause an intelligent person to feel in any way emotional? Thomas Bisse, an eighteenth-century English theologian, believed that divine intercession was responsible for music's ability to move us. He expounded his views in a sermon on September 7, 1726:

The musick is not in the instrument, nor in the ear. The instruments and their furniture, we see, are mere matter, wood, metal or string, the work of the crafts-man; which neither feel, nor hear, nor of themselves move nor send forth any sound. And the ear, though it seems to hear, and is the work of the Divine arti-ficer, is still not an instrument; and though of finer texture and materials than the former, is in itself altogether as insensible. But by the cooperation of both these instruments, natural and artificial, God works in us to hear all we hear and enjoy as musick.

In many ways, Bisse was ahead of his time. His suggestion that emotion in music was not produced by the music itself prefigured the ideas of Igor Stravinsky by more than two centuries. Stravinsky, regarded by many as the greatest composer of the twentieth century, caused an uproar when he stated that music was powerless to express anything. The popular understanding that music can intrinsically express emotion is, according to him, "an illusion and not a reality." Logically, he must be right: music is, after all, too abstract to express anything. It merely tricks a responsive part of the brain into believing that something emotional has happened. There is nothing particularly odd about this; you have only to look at a simple optical illusion to realize how easy it is to deceive the brain. So we may feel nostalgic if music makes us think of a place we used to know, or we may smile if we hear a piece that prompts happy memories, but these emotions are triggered not by the music itself but by the events of our lives with which the music has become associated.

What causes the brain to react emotionally to music? We don't really know, although many believe that it has something to do with the heart. The heart, after all, has a continuous beat like music, and it speeds up when we get excited and slows down during periods of calm. But scientists are still a long way from understanding the complexities of the human brain – and perhaps that is a good thing. Just as conjur-ers' tricks lose their magic when we know their secret, music is often most enjoyable when we allow the brain to produce its emotional

The composer Igor Stravinsky reading a score. "Music," he said, "is far closer to mathematics than to literature – not perhaps to mathematics itself, but certainly to something like mathematical thinking and mathematical relationships."

Opposite Putting meaning into music? The celebrated cellist, Jacqueline Du Pré (1945–87), was regarded during her lifetime as one of the world's most communicative musicians.

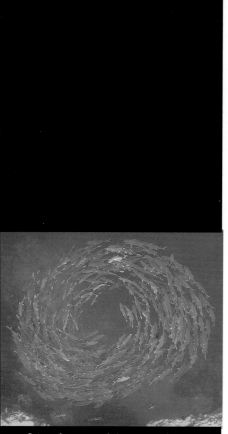

Scientific research has recently revealed that fish respond to music: shoals of ocean fish actually "dance" in circles to the sound of Beethoven relayed to them on waterproof speakers dangled below the water's surface.

responses as freely as possible without questioning too closely where these responses are coming from.

Humans are apparently not the only creatures to respond positively to classical music. This may have come as some surprise to the French philosopher Voltaire who expressed the view in his *Philosophical Dictionary* of 1764 that some creatures are adversely affected by music. "The harmony of a concert, to which you listen with delight," he wrote, "must have on certain classes of minute animals the effect of terrible thunder; perhaps it kills them." It is not uncommon for people to claim that their pets enjoy the sound of classical music, and even some plants seem to show an instinctive liking for music. In a controlled experiment at Annamalai University in India, for example, balsam plants subjected to recordings of lute music grew taller and lusher than unserenaded balsams. Rice plants, too, were shown to produce considerably higher yields than average when grown to the sound of music. Stranger still, research carried out at the University of Denver during the early 1980s found that plants actually preferred classical music to rock music! Those subjected to rock and heavy metal grew either freakishly high or remained stunted, and they all died within two weeks. By contrast, plants grown under otherwise identical conditions, but to the strains of Handel and Bach, flourished and even leaned toward the source of the music.

The Meaning of Music

"Yes, I hear the trumpet, and I hear the tune, but I'm still not sure what I'm supposed to be listening for. What does it all mean?" Being human, we all suffer from the irrepressible need to ascribe meaning to everything, and music is no exception. Works with descriptive titles such as Vivaldi's *The Four Seasons* or Rimsky-Korsakov's "Flight of the Bumble Bee" trick us into believing that the music itself carries a meaning. Interestingly, pieces with narrative titles have always proved more popular than those without. Vivaldi composed reams of violin concertos, but none so popular as *The Four Seasons*, not because *The Four Seasons* are necessarily his best concertos (he was a remarkably consistent composer), but because the title itself has captured the public imagination in a way that none of his other violin concerto titles ever has. Along similar lines, Beethoven published two piano sonatas in

1802, equally brilliant in their own way. Each bore a long, unpoetic title, leaving no clues to the mood or character of the music. One was called Sonata No. 13, opus 27, No. 1 in E flat; the other Sonata No. 14, opus 27, No. 2 in C sharp minor. Some time after Beethoven's death, the German music critic and poet Ludwig Rellstab attended a concert at which Beethoven's Sonata No. 14 was played. In his review, Rellstab wrote that the music reminded him of "a boat visiting, by moonlight, the primitive landscapes of Vierwaldstatersee in Switzerland." Before long, the work came to be known as the "Moonlight Sonata" and its popularity soared, while its unfortunate companion, Sonata No. 13, is hardly ever played.

Moonlight, by Joseph Wright of Derby, 1792. There's nothing wrong in believing you can hear moonlight in the "Moonlight Sonata," even though Beethoven was not thinking about moonlight when he composed it. In fact, such associations can be a positive advantage as they help to fire the imagination.

Like descriptive titles, lyrics also make a piece seem more accessible. When we listen to a song, the music appears to carry the meaning of the words – but this is just an illusion. If we were to hear the accompaniment alone, or if the vocal line were simply hummed, we would have no idea what the music was intended to mean. In fact, the only way we could guess the meaning of the song would be from the overall mood of the music, for wistful or reflective texts are generally set to slow music in the lower register of an instrument or voice, while poems or words expressing panic or turbulent emotions are set to fast music using voices and instruments at the higher end of their range. But why should we associate low, slow music with calm, and fast, high music with tension? The most likely explanation is that music reflects the way the human body works. A calm, relaxed person, for example, will have a slower heartbeat and will talk more slowly and at a lower pitch than someone who is tense, angry or frightened.

In short, we should not expect to find meaning in music. A sonata by Beethoven has no meaning at all. It is an abstract noise. Yet we can make sense of it by introducing elements common to our experience (human emotions, moods, moonlight and so on) that at least help us believe that we have understood the meaning of sound.

Chapter 2
The Elements
of Music

Musical people are so very unreasonable. They always want one to be perfectly dumb at the very moment when one is longing to be absolutely deaf...
Oscar Wilde, *An Ideal Husband*, 1895

According to the famous contemporary composer, Hans Werner Henze, there is "no such thing as an unmusical person." People who profess not to like music have probably not made much of an effort with it in the first place. Certainly effort plays a part in enjoying all music but perhaps classical music more than other forms. To enjoy music properly the enthusiastic listener needs a basic understanding of what classical music is as well as an ability to recognize those instruments and other elements from which great music is created. At a concert, listeners who know what they are looking at will get more pleasure out of what they are hearing.

The London Philharmonic Orchestra, organized according to Stokowski's standard "American seating plan."

The Orchestra

Orchestral music is in many ways less demanding to listen to than music for solo instruments or chamber groups. Different instruments have very varied characters, so it is far easier for the ear to pick out inner lines of counterpoint (see p. 36) when a work is played by several instruments than when all the lines are played by just one instrument, or several of the same type. But it isn't only to provide instrumental clarity that composers write for the orchestra: by using different combinations of instruments, they can effectively paint colour on to their black and white musical pictures. It is this richness and variety of sound that makes the orchestra such a versatile instrument.

Suppose, for example, that a composer wished to write a piece consisting of one note, played loudly for exactly one second. If this rather unlikely and unattractive work were written for solo piano, there is obviously only one way the piece could sound. Composed for a trio consisting of an oboe, a flute and a clarinet, however, there would be seven different ways of scoring the work: clarinet solo, oboe solo or flute solo; flute and clarinet, flute and oboe, oboe and clarinet; or all three together. For a string quartet there would be fifteen different options, while for an ensemble of thirteen different instruments (like Mozart's famous Wind Serenade, K. 361) the composer would be confronted with a dazzling array of 8,191 different ways to score the single note. Clearly, the number of different sounds a whole orchestra can make is almost limitless, and it is probably for this reason that many composers have reserved their most important and lofty musical ideas for the orchestra. The orchestra stands out as a unique collective instrument, posing the fiercest challenge to the composer and providing the listener with music's most richly rewarding medium.

Before World War II, the seating plan of an orchestra was adapted to the individual needs of each concert. The number of musicians in each section was taken into account, as well as the acoustics of the concert hall or church where the music was being played and the sound of individual players. Much to the detriment of orchestral music as a whole, the seating plan of a regular symphony orchestra has now been standardized. This seating plan, which is sometimes referred to as "the American seating plan," was invented by the British–American conductor, Leopold Stokowski, and worked particularly well in his concert hall in Philadelphia. The main feature of this plan was to position all the violins to the conductor's left and the cellos and double-basses to the right. Ironically, Stokowski experimented more than any other conductor with a wide range of different orchestral configurations and would never himself have agreed that one seating plan was ideal for all places and all occasions.

At a standard orchestral concert, it is best to avoid seats too close to the orchestra (where the nearest instruments sound overly prominent), high up above the orchestra (where the brass instruments are disproportionately loud) and too near the walls (where the sound waves bounce around). In most concert halls, the ideal spot is about thirty feet behind and slightly to the left of the conductor, and, where possible, with your head about three feet above that of the conductor.

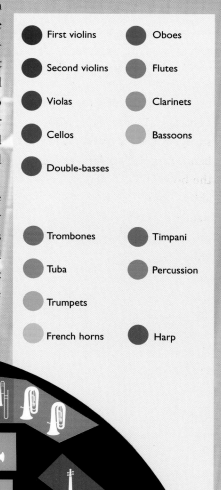

First violins

Second violins

Violas

Cellos

Double-basses

Oboes

Flutes

Clarinets

Bassoons

Trombones

Tuba

Trumpets

French horns

Timpani

Percussion

Harp

23

STRINGS

The string section is the backbone of the orchestra, and there are more string players in an orchestra than any other type of musician. An orchestra without strings is not an orchestra but a band. In a well-trained orchestra the bows in each string section always move together. A standard number of strings for a modern symphony orchestra would be:

First violins	12
Second violins	12
Violas	10
Cellos	8
Double-basses	6
TOTAL	48

VIOLIN AND VIOLA

sound: human, plaintive, lyrical, resolute

remarks: the viola is a larger, alto version of the violin. The best instruments were made between 1600 and 1800 in Cremona, Italy, by the Stradivari, Amati and Guarneri families

concertos: (violin) Beethoven, Mozart, Mendelssohn, Bruch, Brahms, Paganini, Sibelius, Elgar, Prokofiev; (viola) Berlioz, Bartók, Hindemith, Walton

When a man is not disposed to hear music, there is not a more disagreeable sound in harmony than that of the violin.
Richard Steele, *The Tatler*, April 1, 1712

That instrument of mixed sex, this hermaphrodite of the orchestra.
Thomas Beecham of the viola, *A Mingled Chime*, 1944

CELLO

sound: sturdy, warm, heart-rending, subtle

remarks: the mainstay of the bass section of the orchestra. Full name: violoncello

concertos: Boccherini, Schumann, Dvořák, Elgar, Shostokovich

The cello is like a beautiful woman who has not grown older, but younger with time, more slender, more supple, more graceful.
Pablo Casals, *Time*, April 29, 1957

PERCUSSION

DOUBLE-BASS

sound: gruff, haunting, threatening, resonant

remarks: before c.1760, usually used to double the cello part an octave lower. The deepest of the strings

concertos: Bottesini, Tubin, Koussevitzky

A dangerous rogue-elephant.
Charles Villiers Stanford of the double-bass, quoted in Hughes and Van Thal, *The Music Lover's Companion*, 1971

The percussion section has the potential to be the largest in the orchestra: literally hundreds of different percussion instruments exist. There are those sounded by striking or shaking a membrane – drums and tambourines for instance – or those that involve hitting a plate or bar of wood or metal, such as cymbals, triangles, castanets and xylophones. Some are tuned instruments and others are not. Before the twentieth century, only a limited number of percussion instruments were regularly used in the orchestra, of which the kettledrums or timpani were the most common.

TIMPANI (kettledrum)

sound: tuned (bass-tenor)
regular in orchestra from: c.1800

BASS DRUM

sound: biggest and loudest drum
regular in orchestra from: c.1840

TRIANGLE

sound: ting, ting
regular in orchestra from: c.1770

BRASS

SIDE DRUM, MILITARY DRUM, TOM-TOM ETC.

size: various types and sizes of smaller drums
regular in orchestra from: various points in the nineteenth century

There is no instrument the sound of which proclaims such vast internal satisfaction as the drum.
George Meredith, *Sandra Belloni,* 1886

The noisy drum hath nothing in it but mere air.
Thomas Fuller, *The Holy State, the Profane State,* 1642

HARP

sound: often used to enrich harmonies
regular in orchestra from: 1840

KEYBOARDS

remarks: the piano is rarely heard in the orchestra although it has appeared more frequently since the 1920s. Harpsichords and fortepianos were regular features of Baroque and early Classical orchestras, however. Before the existence of conductors, orchestral music was directed from a keyboard instrument, which simply filled in the chords.

The brass is the noisiest section of the orchestra and, for that reason, is always seated at the back. French horns and trumpets were the first brass instruments to join the conventional orchestra during the Baroque period. Later came the trombones and tubas. During the eighteenth and nineteenth centuries the brass section was mostly used to strengthen the general sound, and seldom (with the exception of horns) employed for orchestral solos. Associations with military music are often unavoidable.

FRENCH HORN

sound: male countertenor, mellow, distinct, distant
siblings: horns in F and B flat, usually combined as a double-horn
regular in orchestra from: c.1700
concertos: Mozart, Haydn, Richard Strauss, Hindemith

The horn, the horn, the lusty horn.
Is not a thing to laugh to scorn.
William Shakespeare, *As You Like It*, 1599

Dieu! que le son du cor est triste au fond du bois!
(Lord, how sad is the sound of the horn deep in the woods!)
Alfred de Vigny, "Le Cor," from *Poèmes Antiques et Modernes*, 1826

TRUMPET

sound: bright, fresh, brassy, optimistic
siblings: cornet, piccolo trumpet, bass trumpet
regular in orchestra from: c.1680
concertos: Haydn, Hummel, Shostakovich

At tuba terribili sonitu taratantara dixit.
(And the trumpet with a terrible noise blared "taratantara")
Quintus Ennius, *Annales*, c.175 BC

For if the trumpet give an uncertain sound, who shall prepare himself to the battle?
Corinthians I, chapter 14, verse 8

TROMBONE

sound: rich, manly tenor, reasonable, sombre
siblings: alto trombone, bass trombone, double-bass trombone
regular in orchestra from: c.1800
concertos: Tomasi, Wagenseil, Rimsky-Korsakov

Trombones are too sacred for frequent use.
Attributed to Felix Mendelssohn

Many a sinner has played himself into heaven on the trombone, thanks to the Salvation Army.
George Bernard Shaw, *Major Barbara*, 1907

WOODWIND

TUBA

sound: flatulent, bass, noisy

siblings: Wagner Tubas (tenor and bass), euphonium (tenor), sousaphone (double-bass)

regular in orchestra from: *c.*1840

concertos: Vaughan Williams, Hoffmann

The tuba is certainly the most intestinal of instruments, the very lower bowel of music.
Peter de Vries, *The Glory of the Hummingbird*, 1974

For the next few days I produced a series of noises so dreadful and so sordid that a rumour went about in the neighbourhood that I was keeping a live elephant in the bath.
Gerard Hoffnung on learning the tuba, *Music Club*, BBC broadcast, 1954

Flutes, oboes, clarinets and bassoons are the most common woodwind instruments of the modern orchestra. Baroque orchestras often used recorders instead of flutes. Each woodwind instrument is made in different sizes. There are at least five different sizes of oboe, for example, while three sizes of clarinet (the bass, the B flat and the E flat) are in common orchestral use. Despite their name, most modern woodwind instruments (with the exception of bassoons) are no longer made of wood but of a variety of other materials.

FLUTE

sound: airy, mellow, sensual, clean

siblings: piccolo (sopranino), alto flute, bass flute

regular in orchestra from: *c.*1700

concertos: Vivaldi, Mozart, Mercadante, Nielsen

The flute is not an instrument that has a good moral effect – it is too exciting.
Aristotle (384-22 BC), *Politics*

When the young men serenaded only the flute was forbidden. Why, I asked. Because it was bad for the girls to hear the flute at night.
Ernest Hemingway describing the Abruzzi peasantry in *A Farewell to Arms*, 1929

OBOE

sound: thin, reedy, clear, incisive
siblings: *oboe d'amore* or *hautbois d'amour* (alto), English horn or cor anglais (tenor), heckelphone (bass)
regular in orchestra from: *c.*1650
concertos: Bach, Mozart, Richard Strauss

I used to compose like the devil in those days, chiefly for the hautboy, which was my favourite instrument.
George Frideric Handel, referring to his youthful chamber works

All first oboists are gangsters. They are tough, irascible, double-reed roosters, feared by colleagues and conductors.
Harry Ellis Dickson, *More Dolce Please*, 1969

CLARINET

sound: mellow, warm, rich, soporific
siblings: E flat clarinet (sopranino), alto clarinet or basset horn, bass clarinet, double-bass clarinet
regular in orchestra from: *c.*1770
concertos: Mozart, Nielsen, Finzi, Copland

The clarinet is suited to the expression of sorrow even when it plays a merry air. If I were to dance in prison, I should wish to do so to the accompaniment of the clarinet.
André Grétry, *Mémoires*, 1789

Clarionet, n. An instrument of torture operated by a person with cotton in his ears. There are two instruments that are worse than a clarinet — two clarionets.
Ambrose Bierce, *The Devil's Dictionary*, 1911

BASSOON

sound: bass, gruff, foolish, plaintive, rustic
sibling: double-bassoon, also known as the contrabassoon (very bass)
regular in orchestra from: *c.*1700
concertos: Vivaldi, Mozart, Weber, Hummel

The bassoon in the orchestra plays the same role as Gorgonzola among cheeses — a figure of fun.
Cecil Gray, *Notebooks*, 1989

The Wedding-Guest here beat his breast,
For he heard the loud bassoon.
Samuel Taylor Coleridge, *The Ancient Mariner*, 1798

29

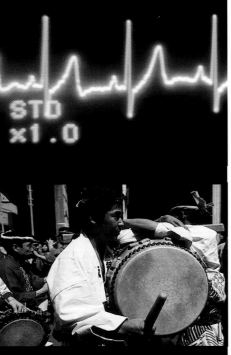

An electrocardiograph printout showing a normal heartbeat. The human heartbeat influences our understanding of musical rhythm.

Pure rhythm: men in traditional dress playing taikos (Japanese drums) during a festival in Choshi, Chiba, Japan

Rhythm, melody and harmony are the three main ingredients of music and good music is always a careful combination of all three. Listening for any of these elements in isolation is not a good idea – it is like trying to understand someone's facial expression by looking only at their eyes. The following brief descriptions will provide the listener with a basic understanding of some of the most common ways in which composers have, over the centuries, used these vital constituents to create moving and inspiring works of classical music.

Rhythm

When we talk, we linger over some words and hurry over others, accenting the important points in a way that gives meaning to the phrase as a whole. Music works in the same way: it too can be divided into phrases, and some notes will be emphasized more than others. The way these notes are arranged in time is known as rhythm.

Rhythm is probably the most basic aspect of music. Although it can exist on its own – in African tribal drumming, for example – rhythm without melody or harmony is very rare in classical music. In fact, it wasn't until the twentieth century that composers such as Edgard Varèse (in his *Ionisation* for thirteen percussion instruments, 1929) set out to challenge the traditional culture of western music by forgoing melody and harmony in favour of pure, unpitched rhythm.

Another important aspect of musical timing is the beat. Beat and rhythm are not quite the same thing. The beat is a regular, metered pattern while rhythm refers to the specific organization of note lengths within each musical phrase. Pieces with the same beat can have completely different rhythms. Waltzes, for example, are dances in three-time (that is to say, the beat is divided into groups of three, with an accent on the first beat: ONE two three, ONE two three), but this does not mean that every waltz will have an identical rhythm – as a comparison of the openings of three Chopin piano waltzes (**CD Tracks 2–4**) will make clear.

Whereas drums and other percussion instruments are almost always used in popular music to maintain a steady beat, they are more often used in classical music to punctuate or underline a rhythm as it is established by tuned instruments. Even without the drums, the beat is quite simple to hear in classical music: by tapping your fingers in time to the music you can usually perceive the beat. If beat refers to the regular repetition of events, then there is beat to the universe and to our everyday lives. There is beat to the cyclical repetition of seasons, months and days just as there is beat to the most fundamental human activities: breathing, walking, the rise and fall of our hormones and — most obvious of all — the pumping of our hearts.

Listening to the beat of a piece can often make even the most complex works of classical music seem more accessible, but don't worry if occasionally you find you can't follow it: sometimes composers deliberately set out to obscure the beat altogether, perhaps to create a sense of timelessness or space. It is quite impossible, for example, to tap your fingers to the famous opening of Wagner's *Tristan and Isolde* (**CD Track 5**), however much you know about music.

In most classical music the beat is regularly speeding up or slowing down; this flexible playing is known as "rubato." It is partly these fluctuations in speed or "tempo" that make classical music so expressive. Tempo marks on the score came into common use only in the eighteenth century, and were often written in Italian. The most common terms for tempo are listed below right.

In addition to rhythm, beat and tempo, there is a broader and more subjective measure of time known as the pulse. The pulse refers to the rate at which musical events occur. Compare the slow pulse of Debussy's *Rêverie* (**CD Track 10**) with the rapidly changing themes and motifs of his "Jeux de vagues" (**CD Track 34**).

Melody

The melody or tune is the real soul of music. Not only does melody bring to a piece of music much of its defining character but, in its repetition and transfiguration, melody is the most recognizable feature of musical form. A melody is made up of one or more musical phrases that weave in and out of a composition. Composers often elaborate on one part of a melody (known as a theme), repeating and varying it throughout the piece.

Melody can hardly exist without rhythm, and it is rare in classical music to find it without harmony, partly because the shape and structure of any melody tends to create its own rhythm and to suggest its own harmonies. Perhaps the nearest thing to rhythmless, harmonyless

Detail of a waltzing couple from a watercolour by W. Gause.

TEMPO MARKINGS

adagio Expansive/slow

allegro Lively/quite fast

andante At a moderate speed

largo Broad/slow

lento Slow

maestoso Majestic/grand

presto Fast/very fast

vivace Lively/fast

Monks singing melodic plainchant, which has no harmony or beat; from the *Psalter of Henry VI, c.1430.*

melody is the monastic plainchant of the Middle Ages. Plainchant does have a rhythm of sorts, but it isn't metered and therefore has no steady beat, following instead the irregular patterns of prose speech.

The art of listening depends partly on being able to recognize a melody, and one of the best ways of doing this is to try to sing it. Singing helps not only to focus on the overall musical shape and character of a piece, but to identify specific themes as well. It is usually quite easy to hum along to the music of composers such as Beethoven, Mozart, Schubert, Bach and Handel; but sometimes it is more difficult to be certain what constitutes a melody and what does not, particularly in the works of later composers like Wagner, Liszt, Sibelius, Bruckner and Mahler. These and many other composers of the late nineteenth and early twentieth centuries developed a style of "endless melody" – tunes and themes that have no clearly identifiable start or finish, but grow almost organically out of one sound and evolve into another.

During the mid- to late-nineteenth century, certain composers began to use musical themes to represent specific non-musical concepts. Berlioz was one of the earliest Romantic composers to experiment with this idea. In his *Symphonie fantastique*, he labelled one important theme the *idée fixe*. Berlioz intended the theme, which appears in various guises throughout the work, to represent "the obsessive image of the hero's beloved." Wagner was another composer to ascribe meanings to musical themes. In the four musical dramas known as *Der Ring der Nibelungen* (The Ring of Nibelung, 1851–74), different leitmotifs are used not only to portray different characters, but also to signify moods, symbols, concepts and inanimate objects such as Fate, Woe, the river Rhine, Redemption, a sword, a dwarf's curse and a pile of gold. His system of leitmotifs is so rich that it creates complex layers of meaning. For example, at the same time as a character expresses his distaste for someone, the orchestra could be playing the theme representing Love, implying that the character is not divulging what he truly feels. It is important to remember, however, that it is only in special instances that composers attached particular significance to a theme: in general, themes have no meaning other than that which we ourselves ascribe to them.

Different styles of melody have also evolved over the centuries to suit different functions. Religious music, for example, usually sounds quite distinct from secular music. Musical instruments were banned in most churches throughout the Middle Ages, so all melodies had to conform to the limitations of the human voice, and hymns had to have an easy tune so that congregations with no musical training could sing them. Furthermore, reverberative ecclesiastical acoustics meant that certain types of fast, complicated music would sound muddled in a church. It was also considered improper in Medieval times for singers to flaunt their musical skills during worship, so church music was sober in tone. The sort of melody you might expect from a hymn is thus very different from one composed, say, for dance music, which needs a lively rhythm and light-hearted tune.

Melody, of whatever type, is the most vital and engaging aspect of music. To Haydn it was "the charm of music," to Mozart "the very essence of music," and to the French composer Charles Gounod, melody represented "the unique secret of his art."

Top Portrait of Hector Berlioz whose *Symphonie fantastique* was inspired by his love for the Irish actress Harriet Smithson, *above*. The two eventually married, but separated after Harriet's long, alcoholic decline.

Harmony

It is very unusual in classical music to find all instruments playing the same tune at the same time. The melody is usually accompanied or underpinned by chords, and this combination of sounds is known as harmony. Harmony is defined as the simultaneous sounding of two or more notes, and although in everyday English the word "harmony" has acquired a positive meaning, in music harmonies can sound either pleasant (concordant) or clashing (discordant).

Guetiges Licht (Kindly Light) by Johannes Itten, 1963. Itten drew a parallel between harmony in music and harmony in colour. According to his theory, "Two or more colours are in harmony if they yield a neutral grey when mixed."

Composers use harmony to bring character and colour to a passage of music. By changing the chords underneath a tune, a composer can alter the whole character of that tune – just as a portrait photographer can transform the character of his or her sitter by changing the background. Perhaps the most famous example of this technique in music can be found in the use of major and minor modes or keys.

The technical difference between major and minor keys is that the third note of a minor scale is a half step, or semitone, lower than that of a major scale. For centuries it has been unanimously agreed that music in a minor key sounds sadder than music in a major key and composers have consequently always used a minor key for their expressions of profoundest grief. **CD Track 6** features two extracts from Schubert's song, "Gute Nacht." The first extract is in a minor key, while in the second both melody and harmony are set in a major key, clearly illustrating the difference between the sombre, depressing feel of the minor and the radiant brightness of the major.

Donna Anna mourning the death of her father, in a production of Mozart's *Don Giovanni.*

Quite apart from defining the overall mood of a piece of music, harmony can be used to achieve all sorts of different effects. By changing the harmonies quickly from one chord to another, for instance, a composer can create a feeling of instability or restlessness. **CD Track 7**, from Mozart's opera *Don Giovanni*, is a perfect example. In this extract, Donna Anna has come upon the body of her father, killed in a duel by her villainous seducer Don Giovanni. The unsettling frequency with which Mozart changes the chords communicates Anna's total desperation and bewilderment, as she sings "Oh Gods, what is this horrible sight before me?...My father! Beloved father! I'm fainting! I'm dying!" The rapidly changing harmonies in Beethoven's "Pathétique" sonata for piano (**CD Track 8**) conjure a very similar sense of instability, but we have no way of really knowing what Beethoven intended to convey in this purely instrumental piece.

By contrast, the two examples on **CD Tracks 9** and **10** show how static or slow-moving harmonies can achieve the opposite effect, that is, to create a feeling of calm and stability. The first track is taken from the famously enchanted Barcarolle from Offenbach's opera *The Tales of Hoffmann*. The second (**Track 10**) features an extract from Debussy's sleepy *Rêverie* for piano, in which the peaceful effects of the slow-moving harmonies again suggest dreamlike calm.

Counterpoint

In classical music, melodies are accompanied not just by sustained chords but by harmonies created from other melodic lines. For example, the strings may be playing one melody while a solo oboe plays a different tune on top. The simultaneous combination of two or more melodies is known as counterpoint. Counterpoint might be described as the accent of musical language, and, because of the almost mathematical difficulties of making musical lines fit neatly together, it is probably the most revealing test of a composer's skill. It is nevertheless a predominant feature in most classical music. In fact it is so ubiquitous that it cannot be said to convey any particular type of emotion. It is as commonly found in tragic music as it is in happy music, in sacred music as in profane, in dances as in marches.

The Return from the Kermesse by Pieter Breugel. Appreciating the detail as well as the overall form of a picture is similar to listening to counterpoint in music.

To understand counterpoint you need to be able to focus on several different instruments at the same time, which is like listening to what one person is saying while other people are talking in the same room. The easiest way to hear counterpoint in orchestral music is to single out the sound of an instrument not playing the main theme and listen to it until it can be heard no more. This way you can hear how the music played by that instrument fits against the main melody. The best instruments to listen for are the oboes, the trumpets or the violins for higher-pitched melodies, and the cellos for the bass. Flutes, clarinets, bassoons and violas can easily be lost in the louder passages, or even muddled with other instruments when they are doubling parts.

The music on **Track 11** of the CD – "I am so proud" from Gilbert and Sullivan's comic operetta, *The Mikado* – is a good example of counterpoint. In this extract, three men are explaining why they don't want to be executed. Only after they have all individually had their say do they attempt to sing all three parts together. It is worth getting to know all the lines separately first, and then trying to extract each part

"I am so proud" – Pooh-Bah, Ko-Ko and Pish-Tush sing in scrambled counterpoint in Gilbert and Sullivan's *The Mikado*.

in turn from the scrambled trio. This is complex counterpoint, but once you can accept the principle of listening to three lines running concurrently, you should be able to recognize counterpoint in any piece of classical music.

Composers' Tricks

Just as painters in the Renaissance learned the art of perspective in order to bring a three-dimensional feel to their flat pictures, so too have composers, through the years, developed a wide range of aural "tricks" to create an illusion of meaning in music. Let us not forget that music is an art and the original meaning of the word "art" was associated as much with guile and deception as with skill and practical ingenuity. The word artificial still means "synthetic" or "contrived," while an artifice (the noun created from the same root) is "a crafty trick" or "an ingenious expedient" – both words come from the Latin for "art," *artis*, with the Latin verb "to make," *facere*.

The following short list of common instrumental tricks gives an idea of some of the ways a composer can bring a sense of meaning into his music by the subtle use of orchestration alone.

Drums and percussion. We tend to think of drums and other percussion instruments as markers of rhythm – and it is true that they are used in general to accent certain beats. But they can also be used expressively. They are a very good way to surprise or shock an audience – a sudden, loud cymbal crash can make listeners jump out of their seats – while gradually increasing the volume and speed of a drum beat always heightens the tension. The sheer physicality of a musician clubbing a kettledrum or clash-

Close-up of a drum roll. Tuned kettledrums or timpani not only provide rhythm: they can be expressive instruments as well.

ing two huge plates of metal together during a concert gives the music an almost tangible presence, and for this reason it can even be helpful to imagine the movements of a percussion player when listening to recorded music.

Composers also use percussion instruments to represent real sounds. A kettledrum, for example, portrays the rumble of distant thunder in Berlioz's *Symphonie fantastique*, gunfire in Prokofiev's *Peter and the Wolf*, and a beating heart in the finale of Tchaikovsky's fantasy overture, *Romeo and Juliet*.

Oboes. Being naturally loud and high-pitched instruments, oboes have long been used for music performed out-of-doors. Like the trumpet, the clarion call of the oboe has also been used to represent hope, because it cuts through dense orchestral textures like a shaft of light shooting through the clouds. In Beethoven's only opera *Fidelio*, for example, the prisoner Florestan is accompanied by the oboe as soon as he sings of hope, and the same effect is evident in the symphonies of Gustav Mahler, where hope and salvation form an important part of his musical message.

Firework display at Green Park, London in 1749, celebrating the Peace of Aix-la-Chapelle. Handel's *Music for the Royal Fireworks*, written for the occasion, was originally scored for twenty-four oboes so that the music could be heard above the noise.

Harps, lutes and celestes. These instruments all have a very soft tone that could never sound brash or vulgar, which may explain why they are so frequently associated with heaven, gods, angels and figures from the spirit world. The celeste is a bell-like keyboard instrument which, as its name implies, is used to evoke celestial images, although it is

probably best known for its first orchestral appearance in the "Dance of the Sugar-Plum Fairy" from Tchaikovsky's ballet, *The Nutcracker*. The harp has been used for centuries to evoke religious images, and both the harp and the lute (which sounds like a cross between a harp and a guitar) figure prominently in church paintings of the Medieval period and the Renaissance. Gluck had the lute accompany mythical gods in his operas, while two harps capture the whirling of an imaginary ball during a dream sequence from the second movement of Berlioz's *Symphonie fantastique*.

Vision of the Seven Angels Playing Harps, from a late thirteenth-century French manuscript.

French horns. Because old-fashioned horns were portable and could easily be played on horseback, they have long been associated with hunting. Primitive horns, which could play only a few notes, were used to signal the sighting of a fox or deer while, in the nineteenth century, horns were sounded to announce the arrival of the post. The horn has since developed into a far more sophisticated instrument, but its old

A trumpet being sounded on the battle-field; sketch by Theodore Géricault.

A figure of fun? Harmen Hals, *The Bassoon Player*, c.1650

links have not been forgotten. Berlioz gives the horn a wistful tune in the Royal Hunt and Storm scene from his opera, *The Trojans*; Vivaldi imitates a horn call with violins in his autumnal hunt scene from *The Four Seasons*; Weber's overture to *Der Freischütz* (an opera about Bohemian hunting folk) is also full of horn music; and Britten, too, used the horn in his setting of Ben Johnson's *Hymn to Diana*, Diana being the goddess of hunting.

Trumpets and cornets. These instruments are loud, clear and portable, making them ideal for military purposes: not only are they sufficiently light to be played on the march, but their sound carries far enough to relay signals on the battlefield. Composers have consequently used trumpets and cornets to represent military themes. Vaughan Williams, for example, echoes the bugle calls across the desolate battle-plains of World War I in his *Pastoral Symphony*, while in Tchaikovsky's *1812 Overture* trumpets are used to evoke the Battle of Borodino (pp. 64–9).

In non-military contexts, trumpet and cornet fanfares have always played a key role in music of pomp and ceremony, and they are frequently used to herald the arrival of messengers, kings, gods and angels. In Beethoven's *Fidelio*, a trumpet fanfare signals the approach of Don Fernando and his men, come to liberate the tortured prisoners of Don Pizarro's bastille. In Handel's *Messiah*, the trumpet accompanies an aria from Part III. The score is marked *pomposo* and the bass sings: "The trumpet shall sound, and the dead shall be raised."

Bassoon. This bass member of the oboe family is often considered as something of a joke, probably because of its unusual shape and rather rough, flatulent sound. It was used by Elgar to depict a drunken Falstaff, and by Prokofiev to portray Peter's grandfather in *Peter and the Wolf*. Some composers – most notably Stravinsky in his ritualistic ballet, *The Rite of Spring* – give the bassoon a bucolic, almost primitive voice.

English horn (cor anglais). Deep and rich in tone, the English horn can often be heard in pieces with a rustic theme. Berlioz used the English horn as the voice of an Italian peasant serenading his mistress in his orchestral work *Harold in Italy*. The instrument is also associated with love, probably because it has a tender, pleading sound. In the eighteenth century the alto oboe, similar in tone to the English horn, was a commonly used instrument known as the *hautbois d'amour* or *oboe d'amore* – the oboe of love.

Strings. Because the human voice and the mechanics of talking and singing are so similar to the way the string instruments work, we tend to feel a particular sympathy for this section of the orchestra. For this reason, composers are often inclined to write their most personal and heartfelt works for the violin, viola or cello.

Tools of the Trade

The cunning deployment of musical instruments is not the only method composers use to imbue their music with an apparent sense of meaning. We have seen how slow-moving harmonies are used to engender feelings of calm and relaxation and how high-pitched noises create moods of tension or hysteria. Fear, surprise, anger, happiness, sorrow, relief and all the other feelings that music seems powerful enough to express are not there by accident, nor were they necessarily arrived at by a flash of inspiration. Composers, however inspired, practice a craft, and, as every good composer knows, there are certain tricks that can always be relied upon to induce a desired expressive effect.

Caricature from 1846 in which members of the audience are overwhelmed by the noise at a concert of Berlioz's music.

Volume. One of the most obvious ways of changing the emotional message of a piece is by changing the dynamic (loudness or softness). Haydn, for example, used an abrupt change of dynamic to shocking effect in his "Surprise" Symphony, in which the opening of the slow movement is suddenly interrupted by an exceedingly loud chord designed to "wake the ladies." Curiously, composers did not generally mark their scores with instructions about volume until well

The American composer John Cage took the rest to its extreme with his completely silent piece, *4'33"*. The instructions on the score are for any instrument or combination of instruments to play nothing at all for exactly four minutes and thirty-three seconds. The "music" thus consists of any sounds made by the audience: a squeaking shoe, or the passing rumble of traffic on the road outside.

into the seventeenth century, when the development of many musical instruments allowed for ever-increasing dynamic ranges that were never possible before. Certain types of music – Gregorian chant and works for the harpsichord – are intended to be played all at one volume.

Rests. Curiously enough, the rest (a silent pause) is one of the most powerful tools in any composer's bag of tricks. Haydn added an extraordinarily long rest at the end of his "Joke" quartet, to give the false impression that the work was over when in fact there were still two bars or measures left to play. Elgar on the other hand used a comma-length silence to reinforce the intensity of a passionate climax from the prelude to his choral work, *The Dream of Gerontius*. Because music is essentially logical, it usually gives us clues as to the direction in which it is heading, but a rest can obscure any sense of what is coming next, and it is this that makes it so manipulative.

Pedal point. This is a term referring to the common technique of sustaining one long bass note under a series of changing harmonies. The term takes its name from the bass pedal notes of an organ (and is sometimes referred to as an organ point), though it is used by all instruments and combinations of instruments. The effects of a pedal point can vary according to which note of the scale is being held in the bass and where in the piece the pedal point occurs. At the beginning of a work it can establish a sense of anticipation, because the longer a note is held the more curious the listener becomes about how and when the note will move. Bach uses pedal point to create an impression of grandeur as well as anticipation at the start of his *St. Matthew Passion*. Toward the conclusion of a piece, however, a long sustained note can have the reverse effect: by creating a sense of stability and affirmation it is used to signal the end of the work.

Scales. A scale is a sequence of notes arranged in either ascending or descending order. We are used to thinking of scales as maddening exercises for beginners learning an instrument, but it is surprising just how much music is constructed from partial or disguised scales. The expressive use of scales is even simpler than we might expect. Music in the descendent (i.e. downward-moving) tends to sound sad or depressing while passages in the ascendant suggest optimism and hope. The reason for this lies, once again, in parallels with human speech patterns: when we are happy our voices tend to be higher than when we are melancholy.

Repeats. By repeating a melody, or sometimes even a whole passage of music, a composer can give structure to a piece. Erik Satie may have taken this point too far with his *Vexations* (1893), a short passage for solo piano repeated 840 times, but in general a repeat serves not only to re-emphasize certain musical points, but also to supply the listener with an anchor or base. A repeat can thus create a sense of emotional stability in even the most turbulent music.

The eccentric composer, Erik Satie. "Before I compose a piece," he said, "I walk around it several times, accompanied by myself."

Tremolo. Tremolo is the Italian word for "trembling" or "quivering." It is produced by repeating a single note very fast (usually with the bow of a stringed instrument), and dates from the seventeenth century, when instruments became sufficiently sophisticated to achieve this effect. The sound usually makes listeners feel tense or fearful. Vivaldi used tremolo to simulate shivering in the first movement of "Winter" from *The Four Seasons* (**Track 30**), while Verdi and Liszt used it to more sinister effect in *Macbeth* and *Czardas Macabre*.

Chapter 3
A New Way
of Listening

JESSICA: I am never merry when I hear sweet music.
LORENZO: The reason is, your spirits are attentive.
William Shakespeare, *The Merchant of Venice*, act V, scene 1

Lorenzo sums up the art of listening in Shakespeare's *The Merchant of Venice* by pointing out that it has as much to do with attentive spirits as with sharp ears. Anyone can listen attentively but how are we supposed to make our spirits attentive as well? And what are attentive spirits anyway? The imagination is what Lorenzo means by the spirits here – not the imagination of words and stories but the imagination of moods and feelings. It is only by allowing your listening imagination to move freely that great music is able to make its effect felt. Lorenzo finishes his speech with a warning against those who do not appreciate music: "The motions of his spirit are as dull as night – Let no such man be trusted."

Concert or Recording?

Many would argue that a well-recorded, state-of-the-art CD offers better sound quality than a concert. Certainly, the balance on CDs is carefully engineered so that the solo instruments of a concerto, for instance, can clearly be heard above the rest of the orchestra, and extraneous noises such as coughs and clunks are edited out. Recordings can be stored and played hundreds of times, while concerts cannot, and therefore recordings provide a much better means of getting to know a piece well. Although the sound at a concert might be truer, the artificially balanced sound of a recording is often purer, making it easier in orchestral music, for instance, to hear the details more clearly. With opera on CD, you can direct the drama in your own imagination, undisturbed by clapping, inaudible words, shuffling audiences or squeaky set-changes. You can dictate exactly how the characters should look, take them out-of-doors, and have them perform acts of magic or murder that not even the most ingenious stage directors could be expected to carry off convincingly; and of course you can choose exactly when it is time for the interval.

The advantages of a live concert are equally compelling. There is something particularly powerful about a concert – probably the unique, ephemeral nature of a live performance, the fact that what you are hearing will never be played in exactly the same way again. Only a CD that self-destructed after one playing might generate the same excitement as a live performance – but for obvious reasons there is never likely to be a market for such a product! Another advantage of live concerts is that they allow you to set your own sound balance: if you wish to hear the harp more clearly you can achieve this quite successfully just by directing your eyes and ears toward that instrument. The physical sight of an orchestra – the coordinated movements and emotions of performers and conductor – can also bring meaning to music. Someone who could see but not hear a concert would be able to

The atmosphere of a concert is created as much by the audience as by the performers. *Top* The Royal Opera House, Covent Garden. *Above* An ecstatic reception at the Royal Albert Hall for Sir John Pritchard at the Last Night of the Proms.

describe the music just by watching the musicians performing it: straining for high notes, relaxing in the slower passages, playing with animation when the music gets faster, with aggression or delicacy at other times, and so on. All these physical signs influence our understanding of what the music is striving to convey and provide a persuasive argument in favour of live music concerts.

Every conductor or musician will interpret a work in a different way, and people who have learned to appreciate a piece of music from a recording are sometimes disappointed when they hear the work at a live concert. In reality, though, most classical music was written with the concert hall in mind, and a recording (however good or exhilarating) is actually a distortion of the composer's original intentions.

The virtuoso violinist Jascha Heifetz enjoyed a long recording career spanning the age of 78s, early electronic recordings and modern stereo.

CDs: Modern or Historical?

The extent to which recorded music has been edited is not widely known. At a recording session, the musicians play each piece four or five times, sometimes more, and it is the producer's job to save the best parts from each performance and edit them together. Editing gets rid of the musical mistakes, as well as any other noises that inevitably occur while musicians are playing. It is rare for a piece to be recorded on to a CD in one complete take: sometimes a record will be edited every three or four notes. Even CDs that claim to be live recordings are usually a patchwork of one or more concerts and rehearsals. The editing process might produce cleaner results, but the spirit of the music, the sort of excitement generated by a good concert, is inevitably lost to a certain extent. Musically, many of the greatest recordings were made before the technology of editing became firmly established – the early recordings of the Russian pianist Vladimir Horowitz, for example, or the stunning unedited performances of the great violinist Jascha Heifetz, which date back to his teens, in the earliest days of commercial recording. The sound on these old recordings is never as clear as modern digital stereo, however, and the choice is often a difficult one to make.

Background Information – Do You Need It?

Knowing a little about a piece before you hear it is one of the best ways of applying meaning to music, and with CD booklets, concert programme notes and good radio presenters, background information is never hard to come by.

Gary Oldman as Beethoven in the 1994 film, *Immortal Beloved*.

The composer. Understanding something of the life of a composer can dramatically enhance your enjoyment of his music. Take Beethoven, for example. It is well known that he began to lose his hearing in his twenties and vainly struggled against encroaching deafness for the rest of his career. It is difficult for us to separate his personal struggles from his music. Beethoven's strength in conquering his despair was nothing short of heroic. Is it just a coincidence then if we think we think we can hear elements of heroism and defiance in his music?

The importance of certain background information can be more easily understood by listening to the short extract on **Track 12** *before* reading on to find out more about it.

The music you have just heard is the very opening passage of Felix Mendelssohn's last string quartet, opus 80 in F minor, written a few months after the death of his older sister, Fanny. Fanny was his closest friend, and as a composer, conductor and pianist of considerable talent herself, she was Felix's fiercest critic as well as his most enthusiastic admirer. On May 14, 1847 she was conducting a rehearsal of her brother's *Walpurgisnacht* in Berlin when she was seized by a paralytic stroke from which she never recovered. The news of her death was clumsily conveyed to Mendelssohn, who immediately collapsed from shock. He regained consciousness, but the loss triggered a severe depression from which, in the few months that remained to him, he never fully emerged.

Mendelssohn was so distraught after Fanny's death that he contemplated abandoning his music altogether. He returned to composing only in the final months before his death, but his last important composition was the string quartet in F minor, composed at

Interlaken in September 1847 as a "Requiem for Fanny."

What's really behind this agitated music is anyone's guess. It is more direct and passionate, though, than almost anything else by Mendelssohn. We know from letters what a desperate state of mind he was in at the time of its composition, and we are aware of the tragic events that inspired the work. Is it too far-fetched, then, to suggest that the extraordinary, whirling opening of the quartet is

Felix Mendelssohn, *left*, and his beloved sister Fanny, *right*.

a musical representation of Mendelssohn's reaction to the news of his sister's death? With all this in mind, listen to **Track 12** again: the likelihood is that knowledge of Mendelssohn's loss will give the piece a profounder, more expressive feel than it had when you first heard it.

The title. If a piece is called "Danse Macabre," "The Flight of the Bumble Bee" or "March to the Scaffold," it is fairly obvious what the music is supposed to be about. But the vast majority of classical pieces have far more cerebral and less descriptive names than these – Prelude opus 2, No. 1 in C sharp minor, for example, or String Quartet No. 6 in F minor, opus 80. The enjoyment of music is not dependent on understanding these titles, but they do give an indication of what type of work to expect and can therefore be helpful when choosing a CD or a concert to attend. A few of the most common forms (prelude, symphony, sonata and so on) are explained on the next page. The opus number is the same as a publication number. Beethoven's opus 1 was thus his first published work. The works of a few other composers are catalogued in different ways, usually with a prefix relating to the person who organized them. Mozart's works were catalogued by Ludwig Köchel and thus bear Köchel numbers instead of opus numbers (e.g. Concerto in D, K. 218). Bach's works are catalogued with BWV numbers and Schubert's with the simple letter D. The key (A major, F minor etc.) refers to the tonality and mode of the piece.

aria A song for solo voice, usually from an opera or oratorio.

concerto A piece for one or more solo instruments and orchestra, usually in three movements. Concertos are normally shorter than symphonies.

Mass A musical setting of the words of the Roman Catholic Mass; usually for unaccompanied voices before 1650, often for soloists, chorus and orchestra thereafter.

overture A short orchestral piece generally preceding an opera or ballet, although from the nineteenth century onward they can be works in their own right.

prelude An introductory, instrumental work, often in an opera. Also a short, self-contained piece for piano or, less often, for orchestra.

sonata A piece in several movements for one or two instruments.

symphony A large-scale work for orchestra, often in four sections or movements. The first movement is generally lively and robust; the second slower, sometimes melancholy; the third faster and in three-time; and the last even more spirited and rhythmic.

The style or period. Music reflects the preoccupations of the era in which it was composed as well as the personality of the composer who wrote it. Works composed during one period, therefore, tend to have certain characteristics in common with one another – such as the combination of instruments, the use of harmony, the function of the music, and so on. There are five main styles or periods of music: Medieval, Renaissance, Baroque, Classical and Romantic, as well as the extraordinary diversification of musical styles that erupted in the twentieth century, which might loosely be described as modernist.

The Medieval era: c.1000–1490. Music developed enormously over the five hundred years between 1000 and 1500. Medieval plainsong or Gregorian chant, the music of the church, can be seen as the starting point of western classical music; certainly it is among the earliest forms of notated music. Outside the church, music was performed in the courts and stately homes of Europe by minstrels, jongleurs and troubadours, but fewer of these secular compositions have come down to us because their creators either felt it unnecessary or – more likely – were unable to commit their music to paper. No one really knows today exactly what Medieval music sounded like, but modern

A Medieval music manuscript.

performers and historians have settled on a highly rhythmic, folksong style for troubadour music of the eleventh and twelfth centuries, while church music is generally sung with as smooth a voice as possible. The most celebrated composers of the Medieval period are Guillaume de Machaut from France, whose secular and religious works earned him a lofty reputation even in his own lifetime; the Englishman John Dunstable, whose religious works were sung all over Europe; Gilles Binchois, a leading figure of the influential Flemish school; and Guillaume Dufay, a cosmopolitan Frenchman whose works cover as wide a range of forms and styles as the number of countries and places where he worked.

The Renaissance: 1490–1620. The Renaissance, which had its roots in Italy, was a period of artistic regeneration. Innovations in music often lag behind those of other art forms, and music of the Renaissance was no exception: the Renaissance period in music is generally thought to have begun some two hundred years after the beginning of the Italian Renaissance of art and literature. Techniques of musical notation were by now well established, and the sophisticated composers of the church were beginning to experiment ever more daringly with the art of writing music in many parts. Key figures of the Renaissance were Thomas Tallis, William Byrd, Christopher Tye, John Sheppard, John Taverner, Thomas Morley, William Byrd, Orlando Gibbons and John Dowland in England, Giovanni Palestrina in Italy, Tomas Luis de Vittoria in Spain, Jean de Ockeghem from Flanders and Josquin des Prez from France. Church music of the Renaissance requires a patient listener. The pace is slow and contrasts are few. Secular madrigals and instrumental music from this period are less cerebral, lighter in tone and, in some ways, easier on the ear.

The Baroque period: 1620–1760. The stylistic distinction between sacred and secular music blurred during this period and it was at this time that the orchestra, as we know it, began to take shape. It was also the age in which some of the standard musical forms started to appear: the

The Minnesinger Heinrich von Meissen and fellow musicians. German Minnesingers, like the troubadours in France and minstrels in England, provided many forms of musical entertainment in the Middle Ages.

The Music Party, painted in the sixteenth century by Pieter Coecke van Aelst.

A Baroque chamber music trio painted by Robert Tournières in about 1700.

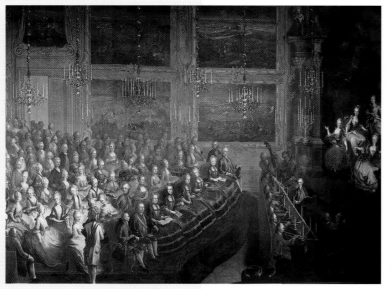

A performance of *Il Parnaso confuso* by the Classical composer Gluck, at the palace of Schönbrunn in 1765.

concerto, for instance, the sonata, the oratorio and the opera. Stylistically, Baroque music falls into two eras: the earlier dominated by Monteverdi, Schutz, Lully and Purcell, and the later period – more florid and richer in style – dominated by the musical giants J.S. Bach, Handel, Vivaldi and Telemann. The later style, with its comfortable rhythms, easily singable tunes and emotional forthrightness, is possibly the easiest musical style of all for listeners to enjoy. The music of the earlier Baroque might seem a little more distant at first but no one could fail to be seduced by the tuneful thrust of Monteverdi's first opera, *L'Orfeo* (1607), or by the heart-rending lament, "When I am laid in earth," from Purcell's opera *Dido and Aeneas*. This is music of considerable emotional intensity and is in no way inferior to the music of later periods.

The Classical era: 1760–1830. Music of the Classical period is characterized by grace and restraint, objectivity and formal elegance. Composers wrote less for the church, concentrating instead on the drawing room and the newly established concert halls. It was in this period that the clarinet established itself as a permanent member of the orchestra and the harpsichord lost out to the newly invented piano. It was also the blossoming age of the string quartet as well as the symphony – a form that developed from the elegance of early Haydn to the lofty grandeur of Beethoven's Ninth (the "Choral"). Beethoven, Mozart, Schubert and Haydn all lived in Vienna at various times in their lives. Two other composers from this period, Gluck and Weber, also had Viennese connections, and both were responsible for pushing the emotional restraint of the Classical style to its limits. But it was Beethoven who really unleashed the Romantic period, with music of unprecedented emotional intensity and innovative and defiant musical form, while the purity and elegance of Mozart's music best epitomizes the essence of the Classical style.

The Romantic period: 1830–1900. During the Romantic period, composers, like writers and artists, began to focus less on formal elegance and more on emotional expression. Other interests at this

time included nature, a theme that had already taken off in Beethoven's Sixth Symphony and Weber's opera *Der Freischütz*; the exotic or the supernatural (evident in the gothic piano style of Liszt, Wagner's operas and the orchestral works of Berlioz); as well as the universal themes of fate, destiny and redemption – explored in the operas of Wagner and the titanic symphonies of Mahler and Bruckner. Not all music of the early Romantic period was as grandiose as this, though: in the early part of the nineteenth century composers such as the Polish pianist Chopin, as well as Schumann and Mendelssohn, were writing music on a more intimate scale. Brahms, hailed by many as "the natural

A Soiree at Franz Liszt's by Josef Danhauser, 1840. Liszt is at the piano, drawing inspiration from a bust of Beethoven. Marie d'Agoult is at Liszt's feet; George Sand (in male attire) sits behind him, next to Alexandre Dumas, and Victor Hugo stands at her shoulder, while Paganini and Rossini look on in admiration.

53

successor to Beethoven" (a title that might have better suited Berlioz), bridged the gap with classical form and lofty expression. In the later part of the nineteenth century, many Romantic composers, especially from eastern Europe, moved toward new styles of nationalist music, inspired by traditional rhythms and folksongs. Leading figures of the nationalist movements included Glinka, Tchaikovsky, Rimsky-Korsakov and Mussorgsky in Russia (see pp. 106–7), Grieg in Norway, and Smetana and Dvořák in Bohemia. Dvořák also helped to sow the seeds of American nationalism in music during a three-year stay in New York (1892–95).

The Violinist, by Toshio Bando, *c.*1930.

The twentieth century. At the beginning of the twentieth century, composers began to explore all sorts of new avenues. Musical nationalism continued to flourish with Rachmaninov in Russia, Vaughan Williams in England and Sibelius in Finland, while Romanticism of a less overtly nationalist strain was singing its swansong in the music of Elgar, Richard Strauss and Puccini. In the meantime, a modernist, discordant musical nationalism was emerging as one of the leading styles of the avant-garde, typified by the works of Bartók, Stravinsky, Prokofiev, Ives, Copland, de Falla, Janáček and Villa-Lobos. Central catalysts for the modernist movement were Debussy and Scriabin, both of whom pioneered new approaches to harmony. Schoenberg and his pupils Berg and Webern, together with Varèse and Ives, were perhaps the earliest composers this century to attempt to impose new rules on all aspects of musical composition, an experimentalism that culminated in the modernist works of Boulez, Stockhausen and Cage. However, many late twentieth-century composers have retained a less radical and more popular approach to music, most notably Barber, Bernstein, Britten, Tippett, Shostokovich, Berio, Henze, Glass and Pärt – all composers who have created new means of musical expression by using the traditional instruments and forms of classical music.

Beauty in Music

We have examined expression and meaning in music but there is another dimension to which all listeners must remain alert if they want to fully enjoy classical music. Beauty is as important to music as meaning and expression but, because it is even more subjective, it is also a more difficult element to qualify. In music, beauty is derived from the purity of the sound of a voice or an instrument, from the shape of a melody,

The Hungarian piano perfectionist Andras Schiff strives for beauty in music – but a good instrument like the one he is playing will always produce a beautiful sound.

the form of a piece, or the melting of one chord into another. A really well-tuned Steinway grand piano, for example, can sound beautiful even if the music it is playing is awkward and unappealing. So it is possible to have beautiful music without expression, just as it is to have expressive music without beauty. In the same way an overcast sky might be beautiful even if it suggests a gloomy mood. This distinction is neatly summed up in the *Oxford English Dictionary*, which defines music as "that one of the fine arts which is concerned with the combination of sounds with a view to beauty of form and expression of emotion."

Mood in Music

One of the aims of this book is to find a way to enjoy all classical music, regardless of its style or date. But to do that we need to identify what it is that all classical music has in common. Music as diverse as the church anthems of Purcell, the symphonies of Beethoven, the string quartets of Bartók or the operas of Philip Glass must have something in common if it is possible for us to enjoy them all.

The element common to *all* music is mood, but whereas many pop songs tend to sustain one mood from start to finish, most classical works involve a flow of constantly changing moods. The genius of the great classical music tradition lies, to a large extent, in its ability to shift from one mood to another within the span of a single continuous movement.

Leonard Bernstein conducting. The facial expressions and movements of a conductor at a concert often tell us about the mood of a piece of music.

Listening for mood in music provides a very good way into a piece, as it allows you to concentrate on the overall sound without having to scrutinize too closely the technical aspects of the work. But reactions to music, as we have already discovered, are highly subjective – there are so many subtly different musical moods that a discussion of any passage of music could elicit fifty different adjectives from fifty different listeners – so we need to find a way of categorizing music simply into a few basic mood types.

Every moment of every piece of classical music, whether it is a harpsichord sonata from the eighteenth century or a computer-generated work of minimalism from the late twentieth century, can be comfortably bracketed into one of three basic mood types. For the purposes of this book, let us call the three mood types PAST, PRESENT and FUTURE. These labels provide logical new definitions for the words "past," "present" and "future," derived from their original meanings. Applying PAST, PRESENT and FUTURE to musical moods is certainly helpful, but remember that the use of these words is poetic, not literal. A fuller explanation follows.

PAST refers to music of a contemplative or reflective nature, music that evokes nostalgia. It is usually slow and lyrical, perhaps with slow-moving harmonies, and is often played at the lower end of an instrument's range. It tends to be very melodic and frequently moves in a descending pattern. Tracks 13 to15 are typical examples of the PAST mood in music.

Track 13 • Brahms, Symphony No. 3 in F major: third movement

The music here comes from the opening of the third movement of Brahms' Symphony No. 3, first performed in Vienna in 1883. The movement is opened by the cellos, whose low register and rich sound are perfectly suited to the yearning mood of this tune. Music in a minor key, marked *espressivo* on the score, and of such warmth, melancholy and plaintive beauty as this, is clearly in the PAST mood.

Track 14 • Debussy, *Suite bergamasque*: "Clair de Lune"

Here the melody meanders slowly downward and, again, there is an emphasis on warmth and richness of sound. The extract is from the opening of "Clair de Lune," the nocturnal movement of Debussy's *Suite Bergamasque* for solo piano. Neither striving forward nor a bald statement of fact, it perfectly captures the wistful nostalgia of the PAST mood in music.

Track 15 • Fauré, *Pavane*

The song-like flute melody from Fauré's magical *Pavane* droops at the end of the phrase in much the same way as the tune from Brahms's Third Symphony (Track 13). Here too the PAST mood is evoked through an unhurried simplicity and a theme with lyrical phrases that move in descending patterns and long breaths.

PRESENT refers to music of an uncomplicated tone that is moving neither forward nor backward. As its name suggests, it is music of the present, a musical statement of fact – a dance or march, for instance, or the recitative of an opera. It is often used to link passages of PAST and FUTURE.

Track 16 • Handel, *Messiah*: Part I

The music in this extract is declamatory and bold, and very much in the PRESENT tense. It is a setting of the Bible text (itself in the present tense) from Haggai, chapter 2, verse 6: "Thus saith the Lord, the Lord of Hosts; Yet once, a little while, and I will shake the heav'ns and the earth, the sea and the dry land; and I will shake all nations and the desire of all nations shall come."

Track 17 • Vivaldi, *The Four Seasons*: "Autumn," third movement

In this extract from the opening of the last movement of "Autumn," the violins imitate the call of hunting horns, a very functional signal for hunters and hounds to follow. In fact, as with many Baroque pieces of this kind, the whole of this "hunting" movement remains in the PRESENT.

Track 18 • Beethoven, Symphony No. 8 in F major: first movement

The bold declaration with which Beethoven opens his Eighth Symphony of 1812 is neither reflective nor forward-looking. It is a simple matter-of-fact musical statement announcing the beginning of the symphony. It proved to be the firm base on which the whole work is founded.

FUTURE is music with forward momentum, music that seems to be questing or moving in anticipation of some future goal. Often featuring rapidly changing harmonies, it is unsettled and not very restful, making the listener wonder where it is leading and how it will be resolved.

Track 19 • Beethoven, Symphony No. 5 in C minor: third movement

The opening of the third movement of Beethoven's Fifth Symphony follows the long, stable music of the slow movement. Here, despite the quietness and the use of cellos and basses, the unsettled rhythm and the effect of frightened tiptoeing puts it into the FUTURE mood. In fact, the passage is typical of FUTURE music: it has a questioning tone, as though the music were trying to peer beyond itself, to get a glimpse into the future. There is a definite sense here that something eventful is about to happen.

Track 20 • Liszt, Transcendental Study No. 2

The whole of this piano study is composed in the FUTURE mode. The music is certainly fast and furious, but it is not only this that puts it into the FUTURE: the dissonant harmonies, trembling figurations and the continually unsettled, off-beat rhythms all contribute to the FUTURE momentum as well.

Track 21 • Beethoven, String Quartet No. 15 in A minor: last movement

Despite the almost PRESENT mood of the first violin's bold declamations, the frequent changes in volume, the mercurial rhythms (just try beating time to this one!), the quivering lower strings and the restless movement of chords all add up to a clear example of the FUTURE mood.

Although there is obviously a subjective element to all this, in most instances it is not so difficult to reach agreement as to which mood (PAST, PRESENT or FUTURE) any particular passage of music belongs to. Even if you are uncertain, the very process of thinking about music in this way is in itself an entirely beneficial method of listening; a way of focusing on the sound without losing sight of the music's expressive message. It is a refreshing way of listening to and thinking about music, and can be usefully applied to any piece from any period of western musical history. Remember, in most classical music these three moods are changing around all the time. Only in shorter works (Chopin's Nocturnes, for example), Baroque music or Renaissance church music is it usual for a composer to capture one mood and sustain it, without change, to the end. By thinking of music in terms of these three mood types it is possible to ascribe a broad emotional meaning to all classical music.

Tracks 22 to **27** feature six more examples of the three moods. All are from the opening moments of six different pieces by Beethoven. Beethoven's music defines the boundaries between PAST, PRESENT and FUTURE moods perhaps better than any other composer, as all his works consist of vivid contrasts between the passionate FUTURE, the lyrical PAST and the affirmative PRESENT.

TRACK 22   Piano Sonata No. 8 in C minor ("Pathétique"), second movement: **PAST**

TRACK 23   Symphony No. 1 in C major, last movement: **FUTURE**

TRACK 24   Piano Concerto No. 5 in E flat major ("Emperor"), last movement: **PRESENT**

TRACK 25   String Quartet No. 7 in F major ("Rasumovsky"), first movement: **PRESENT**

TRACK 26   Piano Sonata No. 32, first movement: **FUTURE**

TRACK 27   String Quartet in B flat major, fifth movement ("Cavatina"): **PAST**

Remember, all classical music can be described, however loosely, as expressive of PAST, PRESENT or FUTURE, and the movement from one mood to another is partly what makes classical music – as opposed to rock, jazz or country and western – quite so unique.

Chapter 4

The World of Music through Seven Key Pieces

In truth, there is nothing like music to fill the moment with substance.

Johann Wolfgang von Goethe, in a letter of October 19, 1829

The following pages take a look at seven key pieces by means of musical "timelines" (computerized images of the music as it passes through time), showing the rise and fall of volume and tension as well as the mood and instrumentation of each passing moment. The works are specially chosen from a wide range of periods and styles, from the rapt beauty of Tallis's Renaissance church music to the seminal modernism of Debussy's *La Mer*, with opera, chamber, concerto, solo piano and symphonic styles all observed along the way. The seven pieces are featured on Tracks 28–34 of the enclosed CD.

How to Use the "Timelines"

Starting with Tchaikovsky's spectacular orchestral show-piece, the *1812 Overture*, the seven key pieces have been specially chosen to represent the widest range of classical forms and styles. Musical highlights, corresponding to the timings on your CD counter, are annotated at key points above the timelines, while a computerized image of the music, working on the same principles as a cardiograph, visualizes the rise and fall of volume and the PAST, PRESENT and FUTURE moods of the music (see Chapter 3), as well as giving indications of musical tension and instrumentation. The text above the timelines provides information about many different aspects of the music itself, ranging from the scoring of the piece to details of the composer's life, the background to the music, contemporary history, and other masterworks by the same composer. All of this can be digested in any order, as each part will contribute to a vivid and rounded understanding of the music itself.

How the Timelines Work

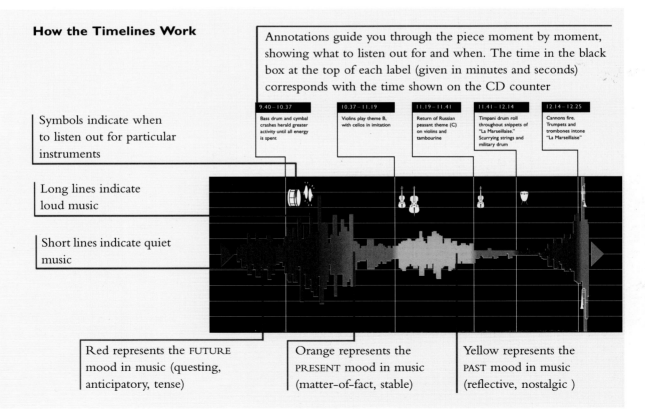

Annotations guide you through the piece moment by moment, showing what to listen out for and when. The time in the black box at the top of each label (given in minutes and seconds) corresponds with the time shown on the CD counter

9.40 – 10.37
Bass drum and cymbal crashes herald greater activity until all energy is spent

10.37 – 11.19
Violins play theme B, with cellos in imitation

11.19 – 11.41
Return of Russian peasant theme (C) on violins and tambourine

11.41 – 12.14
Timpani drum roll throughout snippets of "La Marseillaise." Scurrying strings and military drum

12.14 – 12.25
Cannons fire. Trumpets and trombones intone "La Marseillaise"

Symbols indicate when to listen out for particular instruments

Long lines indicate loud music

Short lines indicate quiet music

Red represents the FUTURE mood in music (questing, anticipatory, tense)

Orange represents the PRESENT mood in music (matter-of-fact, stable)

Yellow represents the PAST mood in music (reflective, nostalgic)

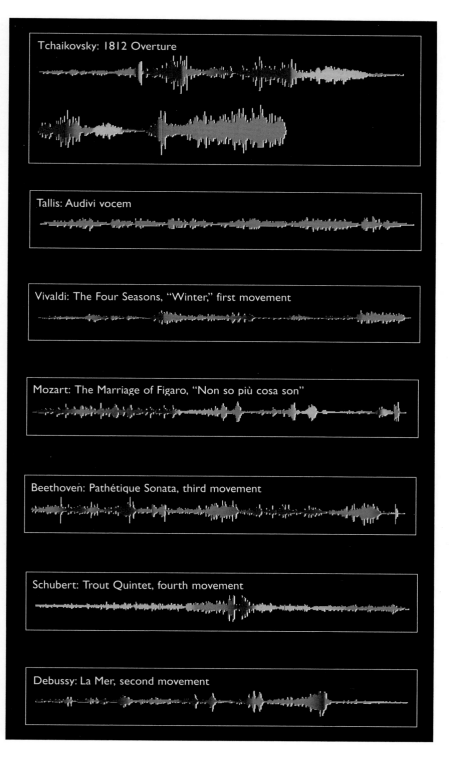

Tchaikovsky: 1812 Overture

Tallis: Audivi vocem

Vivaldi: The Four Seasons, "Winter," first movement

Mozart: The Marriage of Figaro, "Non so più cosa son"

Beethoven: Pathétique Sonata, third movement

Schubert: Trout Quintet, fourth movement

Debussy: La Mer, second movement

Even at a glance, these timelines will tell you about the mood, volume and intensity of each piece. Compare the evident calm of Tallis's *Audivi vocem*, for example, which remains constant in volume and mood from start to finish, with the dramatic changes of Tchaikovsky's *1812 Overture*.

TCHAIKOVSKY'S 1812 OVERTURE

The Overture will be very loud and noisy; I am writing it without affection or enthusiasm, and therefore there will probably be no artistic merit in it.
Pyotr Ilyich Tchaikovsky

Classical music, with the exception of opera and ballet, does not usually have a narrative – but when it does, the listener's job is made unquestionably easier. Tchaikovsky's famous concert overtures, *Francesca da Rimini*, *Hamlet* and *Romeo and Juliet* to a certain extent all follow storylines, but none more so than the great festival overture, the *1812*, which recalls, through vivid music, the events of the Battle of Borodino in which the Czar's troops were narrowly defeated by the invading French armies of Napoleon Bonaparte on their way to Moscow.

The Battle of Borodino, a contemporary painting by Louis François Lejeune.

The Musical Background of the *1812*

The *1812 Overture* was commissioned for inclusion in the Russian Exhibition of 1882 by the conductor, composer and pianist Nikolai Rubinstein (1835–81). Tchaikovsky was asked for a piece that would both commemorate the seventieth anniversary of the Russians' bravery against Napoleonic troops at the Battle of Borodino in 1812, and celebrate the opening of the new Kremlin Cathedral of Christ the Redeemer in Moscow. Tchaikovsky hated this sort of commission and completed the work with bad grace. His integrity as a composer and his genuinely strong personal feelings of Russian patriotism won out in the end, however, and this still critically underrated masterpiece was given its first performance in

Moscow on August 20, 1882. The cathedral itself was destroyed during the Russian Revolution some thirty-five years later, but Tchaikovsky's overture still stands as a monument to Russian imperialist pride and heartfelt Muscovite patriotism.

The Story of the Battle

Relations between the great European powers at the beginning of the nineteenth century were strained by the threatening military manoeuvrings of the French under Napoleon. By 1812, the fragile Franco-Russian alliance had collapsed, and in the spring of that year Napoleon had amassed an army of 453,000 soldiers to invade his Russian foe. The Battle of Borodino was a narrow victory for the French and represented the last serious stand of Russian defence before Napoleon's troops marched on, more or less unopposed, into Moscow.

ORCHESTRATION

Percussion
1 triangle
1 tambourine
1 military drum
1 bass drum
1 pair of cymbals
1 cannon
  timpani
  bells

Brass
4 French horns
2 trumpets
2 cornets
2 tenor trombones
1 bass trombone
1 tuba

Woodwind
2 flutes
1 piccolo
2 oboes
1 English horn
2 clarinets
2 bassoons

Strings
violins
violas
cellos
double-basses

Other
organ (optional)

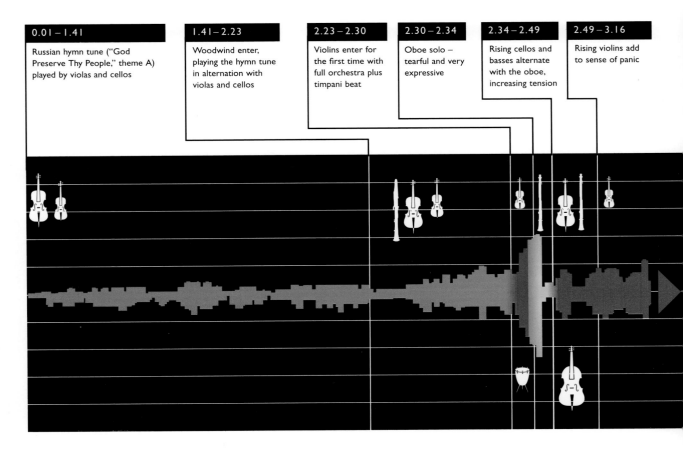

0.01 – 1.41
Russian hymn tune ("God Preserve Thy People," theme A) played by violas and cellos

1.41 – 2.23
Woodwind enter, playing the hymn tune in alternation with violas and cellos

2.23 – 2.30
Violins enter for the first time with full orchestra plus timpani beat

2.30 – 2.34
Oboe solo – tearful and very expressive

2.34 – 2.49
Rising cellos and basses alternate with the oboe, increasing tension

2.49 – 3.16
Rising violins add to sense of panic

Tchaikovsky, photographed in 1890.

Tchaikovsky's *1812 Overture* offers up a prayer for the souls of the 45,000 Russians killed at Borodino. The hymn itself ("God Preserve Thy People") is heard at the opening and recurs in grander form toward the end. Although the music is not specifically marked with a narrative, it isn't hard to imagine the Russians praying, singing bravely, preparing for battle, and celebrating the eventual routing of French troops from the capital. The way in which the French national anthem, "La Marseillaise," gets swallowed up by the sheer volume and grandeur of the "Emperor's Hymn" (14.33) is a clear example of musical symbolism.

Tchaikovsky the Man

Pyotr Ilyich Tchaikovsky was born in Kamsko-Votkinsk, a small Russian mining town in the province of Vyatka. His father was a

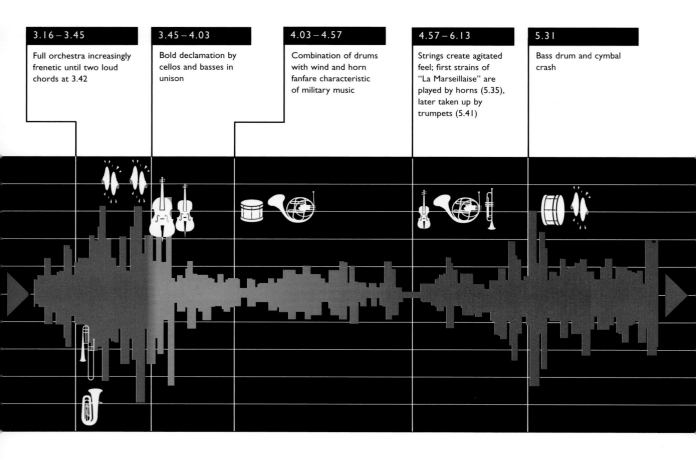

3.16 – 3.45
Full orchestra increasingly frenetic until two loud chords at 3.42

3.45 – 4.03
Bold declamation by cellos and basses in unison

4.03 – 4.57
Combination of drums with wind and horn fanfare characteristic of military music

4.57 – 6.13
Strings create agitated feel; first strains of "La Marseillaise" are played by horns (5.35), later taken up by trumpets (5.41)

5.31
Bass drum and cymbal crash

mining engineer, and despite an early love for music, Pyotr started his professional career as a civil servant. When he first began to compose music he was only five years old, and for his first serious training he had to wait until he could enlist at the St. Petersburg Conservatoire of Music in 1862. Early successes came with his first two symphonies and the First Piano Concerto in 1875 – a work which, in the early twentieth century, was to become the first piece of classical music to sell over a million copies on record. In 1875 he started to correspond with a rich aristocrat, Nadezhda von Meck, who, until an unfortunate misunderstanding in 1890, supported Tchaikovsky financially so that he could afford to devote himself exclusively to composition. Contact between them was always by letter and they never met.

In 1877 Tchaikovsky rashly married Antonina Milyukova, possibly in an attempt to disguise his homosexuality, but the marriage was a

Nadezhda von Meck, Tchaikovsky's patron.

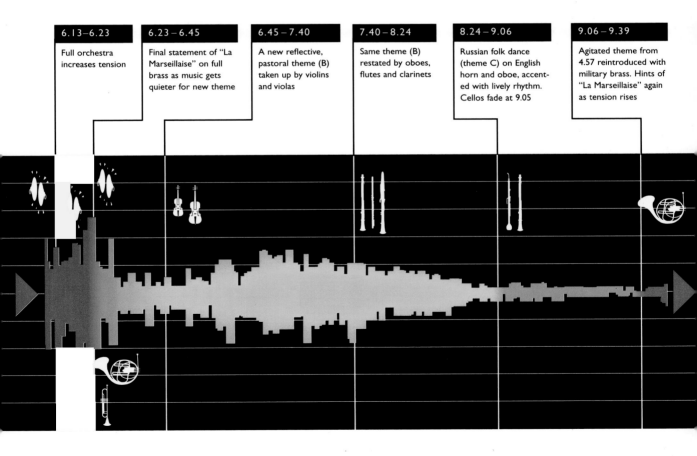

6.13–6.23	6.23–6.45	6.45–7.40	7.40–8.24	8.24–9.06	9.06–9.39
Full orchestra increases tension	Final statement of "La Marseillaise" on full brass as music gets quieter for new theme	A new reflective, pastoral theme (B) taken up by violins and violas	Same theme (B) restated by oboes, flutes and clarinets	Russian folk dance (theme C) on English horn and oboe, accented with lively rhythm. Cellos fade at 9.05	Agitated theme from 4.57 reintroduced with military brass. Hints of "La Marseillaise" again as tension rises

disaster and the composer tried to kill himself only eleven weeks after the wedding. For the rest of his life, despite composing some of his greatest works, Tchaikovsky fell prey to repeated bouts of mental depression until, in the winter of 1893, he succumbed to a fatal dose of self-administered arsenic. Allegations persisted that he was coerced into killing himself by a hastily instituted court of honour committee, following rumours of a homosexual scandal involving the nephew of a high-ranking civil servant; but the official diagnosis at the time was cholera.

Tchaikovsky the Composer

In [Tchaikovsky] I see the greatest, or rather the only, hope for our musical future.

Herman Laroche (1845–1904), Russian music critic

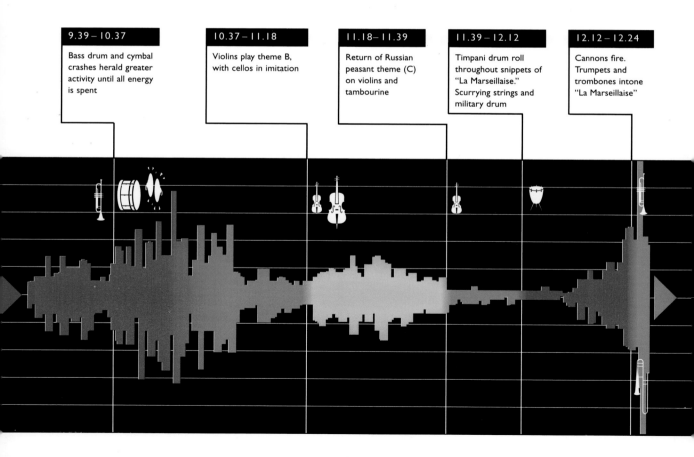

9.39–10.37
Bass drum and cymbal crashes herald greater activity until all energy is spent

10.37–11.18
Violins play theme B, with cellos in imitation

11.18–11.39
Return of Russian peasant theme (C) on violins and tambourine

11.39–12.12
Timpani drum roll throughout snippets of "La Marseillaise." Scurrying strings and military drum

12.12–12.24
Cannons fire. Trumpets and trombones intone "La Marseillaise"

Many would regard Tchaikovsky as Russia's finest composer. His style is rich in Russian melancholy, although the *1812 Overture* is perhaps one of his more jubilant works. His particular strain of wistful melody is derived, in part, from a lifelong love of Russian folk music. His dynamic rhythms also have their roots in folk music, while the purity and grace of his smaller works (the Serenade for Strings, for instance) show the slight influence of his favourite classical composer, Mozart.

As the leading Russian composer of Romantic music, Tchaikovsky was also one of his country's greatest exponents of the difficult art of orchestration. The *1812 Overture* demonstrates a wide range of colourful orchestral effects, from the unusual inclusion of cannons, bells and optional organ to the subtle blending of flutes and English horn for the Russian peasant theme (8.24) and the chilling effect of the whole orchestra descending together in awesome scales at 12.24.

MASTERWORKS

Orchestral

1869	Romeo and Juliet, Fantasy Overture
1875	Piano Concerto No. 1 in B flat minor
1876	Swan Lake (ballet)
1877	Symphony No. 4 in F minor
1878	Violin Concerto in D major
1880	Serenade for Strings in C Major
1885	"Manfred" Symphony
1888	Symphony No. 5 in E minor
1889	The Sleeping Beauty (ballet)
1892	The Nutcracker (ballet)
1893	Symphony No. 6 in B minor

Opera

1878	Eugene Onegin
1890	The Queen of Spades

Chamber and solo

1876	The Seasons, for solo piano
1890	Souvenir de Florence (string sextet)

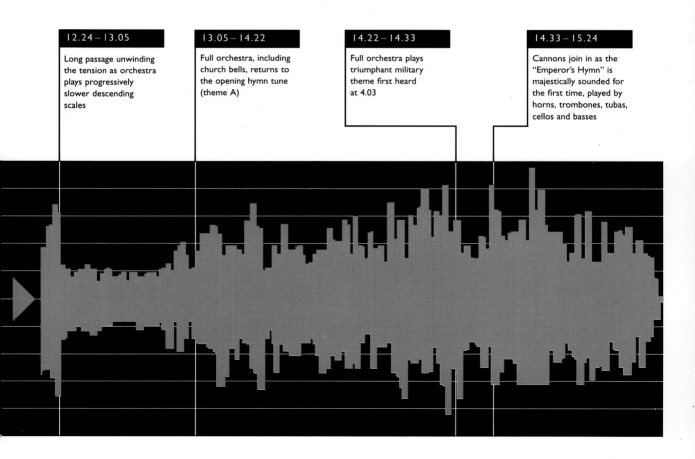

12.24 – 13.05
Long passage unwinding the tension as orchestra plays progressively slower descending scales

13.05 – 14.22
Full orchestra, including church bells, returns to the opening hymn tune (theme A)

14.22 – 14.33
Full orchestra plays triumphant military theme first heard at 4.03

14.33 – 15.24
Cannons join in as the "Emperor's Hymn" is majestically sounded for the first time, played by horns, trombones, tubas, cellos and basses

TALLIS'S AUDIVI VOCEM

...as he dyd lyve, so also did he dy.
In myld and quyet Sort (O! happy Man).
Epitaph to Thomas Tallis at the Church of St. Alfege, Greenwich

Audivi vocem is the eighth respond (a chant or anthem) to be sung during Matins on All Saints Day. Responds or responsories were part of daily service at the Chapel Royal and consisted of alternating sections for soloists and choir. This setting of *Audivi vocem* was one of thirty-four *Cantiones Sacrae*, or Sacred Songs, published in 1575 by Thomas Tallis and his pupil, the composer William Byrd. The volume was dedicated to Queen Elizabeth I, with each composer contributing one song for every year of Elizabeth's reign to date. Responds at this time were sung in church Latin. The text of *Audivi vocem* is as follows:

Monks singing psalms, from the fifteenth-century *Bible of Borso d'Este*.

Respond

Audivi vocem de caelo venientem: venite omnes virgines sapientissime; oleum recondite in vasis vestris dum sponsus advenerit.

Verse

Media nocte clamor factus est: ecce sponsus venit.

Respond

Oleum recondite in vasis vestris dum sponsus advenerit.

Respond

I heard a voice coming from heaven: come, all you most wise virgins; store up the oil in your vessels until the bridegroom comes.

Verse

At midnight the cry broke forth: behold, the bridegroom comes.

Respond

Store up the oil in your vessels until the bridegroom comes.

It was usual — as in the famous earlier setting of the same text by English composer John Taverner — for the solo sections of *Audivi vocem* to be sung by groups of boys with a male voice choir singing the plainchant verses, but Tallis chose to use adult voices instead of boys'. The version on **CD Track 29** is sung by a plainchant choir and four soloists: two female altos, one tenor and one bass. Renaissance church music of

70

this kind is not as dramatic as other forms of classical music, but it expresses a calming spirituality that makes it particularly appealing to the modern listener. The tone, volume and mood are established at the outset and change very little over the course of the work (compare it with Debussy's "Jeux de Vagues," **Track 34**).

Tallis the Man

Born around 1505, Thomas Tallis was one of the greatest composers of the English Golden Age. He lived during the reigns of four successive English monarchs – Henry VIII, Edward VI, Mary I and Elizabeth I – and consequently experienced the religious upheavals of the Reformation and Counter-Reformation, which placed considerable demands on composers of church music. The few surviving contemporary accounts of Tallis describe him as a

Engraving of Thomas Tallis by an unknown artist.

0.01, 0.04, 0.07, 0.15	0.20–0.40	0.40– 1.14
Alto 1, alto 2, tenor and bass enter one by one, each singing "Audivi." This kind of echo was extremely common in Renaissance church music	Listen for the way the four soloists continue to echo each other; they are still singing "Audivi"	A male voice choir continues the respond, singing in plainchant. Plainchant has no metered rhythm: instead it follows the rhythm of the words themselves

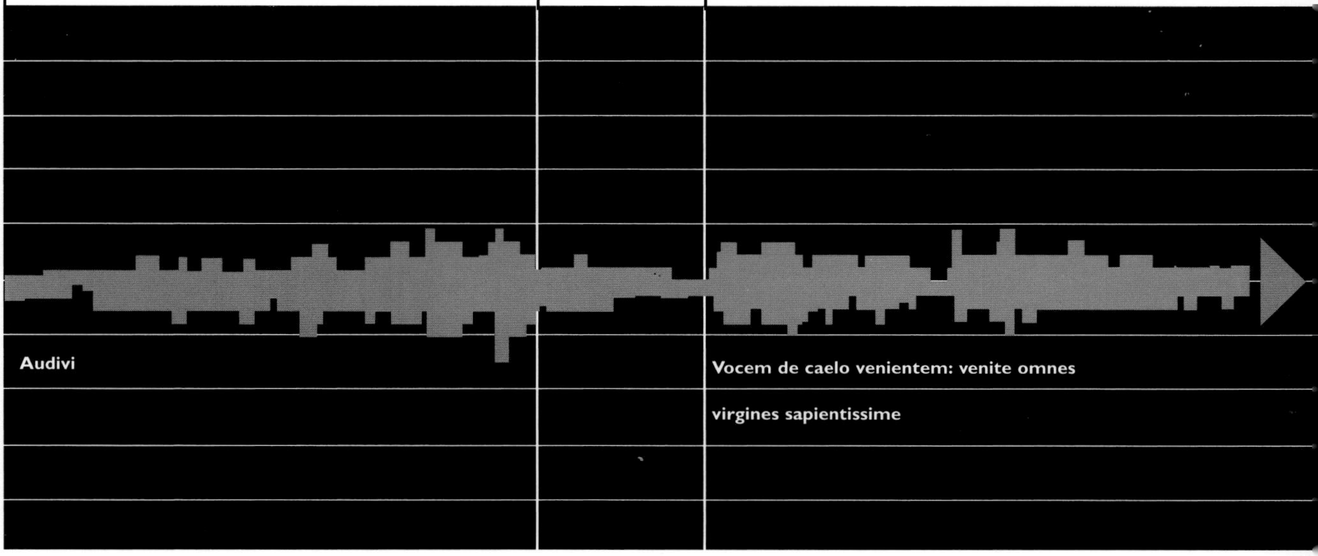

Audivi

Vocem de caelo venientem: venite omnes

virgines sapientissime

Queen Elizabeth I at prayer in the Chapel Royal, where many of Tallis's works would have been performed.

mild and pleasant-mannered man. He was organist at Waltham Abbey until it was dissolved in 1540 and a Gentleman of the Chapel Royal for many years until his death. In 1575, Queen Elizabeth I granted Tallis and Byrd a monopoly to print and publish music. This privilege lasted twenty-one years and turned both composers into wealthy men. Tallis's wife Joan is believed to have survived him by some forty years.

Tallis the Composer

Tallis is dead, and music dies.

Words set to music by William Byrd in his lament on the death of Tallis, 1586

The historical importance of Thomas Tallis has as much to do with the innovation and variety of his style as with his technical and musical

---

1.14–1.43

The third phrase of the respond ("oleum recondite in vasis vestris") rises in pitch, returning to a lower pitch for the final phrase ("dum sponsus advenerit")

1.43–2.02

Alto 2, bass, alto 1 and tenor enter once more, singing the first phrase of the verse

2.00–2.25

Alto 1 is singing a slightly different melody line, rather like a slow hymn, while the other soloists sing counterpoint below

Oleum recondite in vasis vestris dum sponsus advenerit

Media nocte clamor factus est

ingenuity. As religious life in England changed, so too did Tallis's music: from the florid counterpoint of his settings of Latin texts, such as the astonishing forty-part choral work, *Spem in Alium*, to the more sober and restrained settings of his English anthems, following the

Title page of *Cantiones Sacrae*, published in 1575 by Thomas Tallis and William Byrd.

MASTERWORKS

Responsories
Spem in Alium (40-part motet)
Videte miraculum
Candidi facti

Hymns and anthems
Salvator Mundi (first setting)
O nata lux de lumine (for 5 voices)
Remember not
Hear the voice and prayer
If ye love me
Lamentations of Jeremiah
(for 5 voices)

Solo piano
Felix namque (variations on a plainchant melody)

stricter rules laid out by the Anglican church. In general, though, Tallis's style is unostentatious, rapt in mood and settling to the spirit.

2.25 – 3.07

Alto 2 and the tenor form one echoing pair while alto 1 and the bass form another

3.07 – 3.38

The choir takes up the plainchant respond, repeating note for note the last two phrases of the first plainchant section. The piece has a very calm ending

Ecce sponsus venit

Oleum recondite in vasis vestris dum

sponsus advenerit

VIVALDI'S THE FOUR SEASONS
"Winter:" first movement

By the time Vivaldi composed *The Four Seasons* in 1725 he was already enjoying a considerable reputation throughout Europe as a popular composer. The concertos that make up *The Four Seasons* were originally published as the first four of a set of eight violin concertos under

Vivaldi is an old man who has a prodigious fury for composition. I heard him undertake to compose a concerto, with all the parts, with greater despatch than a copyist can copy it.
Charles de Brosse, in a letter of 1739

the title "Il Cimento dell'Armonia e dell'Invenzione" (The Contest of Harmony and Invention). Their popularity has far outstretched the reputation of any other of Vivaldi's 230 violin concertos, and even in his lifetime these pieces were recognized as landmarks in the development of virtuoso violin technique.

The Frozen Lake in 1708, painting by G. Bella.

"Winter"

By adding descriptive titles to many of his works Vivaldi was to some extent following the path of contemporary fashion, but with *The Four Seasons* he went a step further, prefacing each of the concertos with a sonnet, thought to be by the composer himself. On the manuscript score he attached lines of each sonnet to specific passages of his music. The sonnet for "Winter" is as follows (the first movement, **Track 30**, relates only to the first four lines):

Aggiacciato tremar trà neri algenti	Frozen and trembling in the ice cold snow
Al severo spirar d'orrido vento,	With the merciless blast of a stormy wind
Correr battendo i piedi ogni momento;	Endlessly stamping one's feet
E pel soverchio gel batter i denti;	The severe frost making one's teeth chatter
Passar al foco i di quieti e contenti	Days spent by the fire in quiet ease
Mentre la pioggio fuor bagna ben cento	While outside all is drenched by the rain
Caminar sopra 'l giaccio, e à passo lento	Slowly walking on ice, one step at a time
Per timor di cader gersene intenti;	Fearful and trying not to trip and fall
Gir forte Sdruzziolar, cader à terra	Walking boldly now, then slipping and falling
Di nuovo ir sopra 'l giaccio e correr forte	Up again on the ice, going faster and faster
Sin ch'il giaccio si rompe, e si disserra;	The ice at last cracks and breaks into pieces
Sentir uscir dalle ferrate porte	To hear blowing out through the iron gates
Sirocco Borea, e tutti i venti in guerra	The Sirocco, the Bora and all the winds battling
Quest' è 'l verno, mà tal, che gioja apporte.	Such is winter, and yet what joy it brings.

ORCHESTRATION

solo violin
violins
violas
cellos and double-basses
(playing the same line)
organ (usually replaced by
harpsichord)

0.01–0.10	0.10	0.35	0.57
Harpsichord, cellos, double-basses, violas and second violins enter in turn	First violins enter. The score is marked *Aggiacciato tremar trà neri algenti*, indicating that the music is supposed to give the impression of trembling	The solo violin, shown in red, enters stormily (*Al severo spirar d'orrido vento* is indicated on the score) and alternates with string chords at 0.40 and 0.48	The soloist joins the first violins as the whole orchestra builds up the tension: repeated chords become increasingly loud

View of the orphanage in Venice where Vivaldi was music master.

This caricature of Vivaldi is the only authenticated portrait of the composer.

Vivaldi the Man

Born in Venice in 1678 to a musical family of bakers, Antonio Vivaldi rose to great fame and prosperity as a composer, a respected teacher, a virtuoso violinist and a priest. By the end of his life, though, his popularity had diminished so much that he died a pauper at a saddler's house in Vienna. During his lifetime he was noted for his large aquiline nose and flame-red hair, which earned him the nickname "the

1.09–1.21	1.21–1.44	1.44–2.00	2.00–2.17
Theme A. The score is marked *Correr battendo i piedi ogni momento*, and the music actually suggests the noise of stamping feet	Violin solo made up of lots of short scales and phrases, shadowed by a rhythmic bass line	*Tremolando* (quivering) strings alternate with violin solo. The score is marked *Venti* (wind) to imply a shivering cold wind	Return to the opening theme, the tension quietly mounting

Red Priest." According to contemporary sources, he was boastful, snobbish and profligate with his money, and although he was in holy orders for most of his working life, he was by no means always in favour with the church.

Vivaldi the Composer

With over 450 concertos, 70 sonatas, 50 operas and numerous motets and cantatas, Vivaldi's output was singularly prodigious. Most famous of all are the concertos, many of which bear descriptive titles, such as *The Four Seasons*. Stravinsky thought Vivaldi an overrated composer: "a dull fellow who could compose the same form over and so many times over." Many would disagree though. His style is nearly always light, rhythmic and easy to enjoy; there is not a particularly marked stylistic difference between the works of his youth and those of his later years.

MASTERWORKS

Violin concertos
Il Cucù (The Cuckoo)
La Caccia (The Hunt)
La Tempesta di Mare (The Sea Storm)
L'Inquietudine (The Worries)
Il Ritiro (The Retirement)

Other Concertos
Il Gardellino (The Goldfinch) for flute
La Notte (The Night) for flute
Concerto in C major for mandolin
Concerto in C major for two trumpets

Choral
Gloria in D major

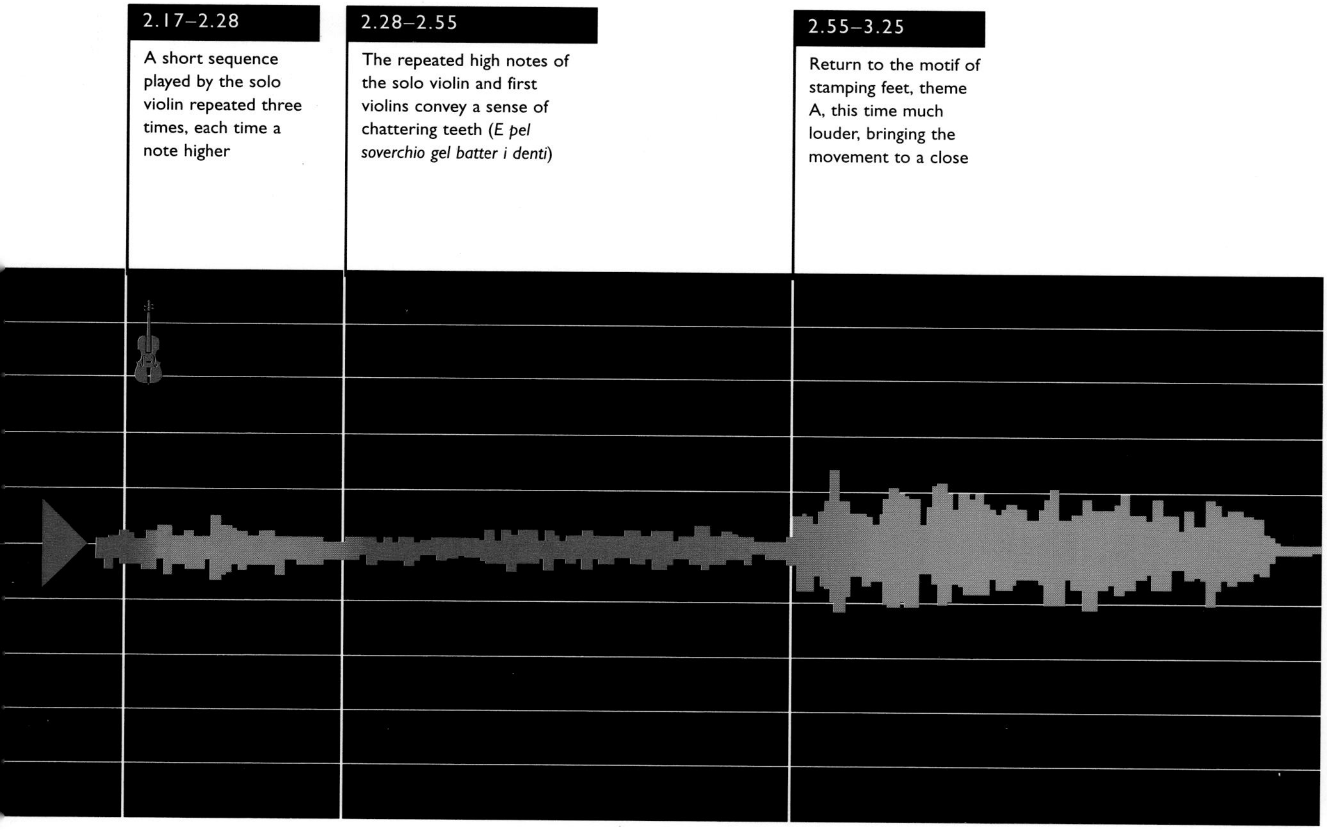

2.17–2.28

A short sequence played by the solo violin repeated three times, each time a note higher

2.28–2.55

The repeated high notes of the solo violin and first violins convey a sense of chattering teeth (*E pel soverchio gel batter i denti*)

2.55–3.25

Return to the motif of stamping feet, theme A, this time much louder, bringing the movement to a close

MOZART'S THE MARRIAGE OF FIGARO

Cherubino's aria: "Non so più cosa son, cosa faccio"

It contains so many beautiful things, and such a wealth of ideas, as can only be drawn from the source of inherent genius.
Review of *The Marriage of Figaro* in the *Wiener Realzeitung*,
July 1786

Mozart and his sister, Maria Anna, at the piano, with a portrait of their mother on the wall behind them. Painting, 1780–81, by J.N. della Croce.

ORCHESTRATION

Cherubino: mezzo-soprano
2 clarinets
2 bassoons
2 horns
violins
violas
cellos
double-basses

Mozart's comic opera of 1786, *The Marriage of Figaro*, is one of the most successful works of the entire operatic repertoire. It was Mozart's first opera set to a libretto by the Italian playwright, Lorenzo da Ponte, and was soon followed by two more da Ponte successes, *Don Giovanni* (1787) and *Così fan Tutte* (1789). Based on the famous French play by Pierre Augustin Caron de Beaumarchais, *The Marriage of Figaro* concerns the vain attempts of a count to exercise his rights over his maid before she gets married and can legally reject his advances. Cherubino, a 13-year-old Adonis who is in love with the countess, and all other women for that matter, is often in the wrong place at the wrong time and his scrapes with the count provide the farce with a particularly comical subplot. His part is always sung by a woman *en travestie* – wearing men's clothes.

Cherubino's Aria

This beautiful song is Cherubino's first aria in Act One. Its purpose is to tell us a little about his character, namely that his panting heart is aflame with irrepressible desires – feelings that are brilliantly captured in Mozart's cleverly palpitating orchestral accompaniment and the breathless line of Cherubino's sung melody. Vocal music can be listened to on two different levels because it contains both words and music, but it is best to try, wherever possible, to understand the text and to relate its meaning to the music. In this instance, a careful reading of the translation of Cherubino's words (opposite) before listening to the music will greatly enhance your understanding and enjoyment of this remarkable aria.

I cannot tell what I am or what I'm doing,

if I'm boiling hot or cold as ice,

every woman makes my colour change,

every woman makes me tremble.

The very words "love" or "delight"

shake me up and churn my breast.

Even talk of love fills me with inexplicable yearnings!

I speak of love when I'm awake,

I speak of it too in my dreams,

to the water, the shadows, the mountains,

the flowers, the grass and the fountains,

to the echo, the air and the winds

which carry away the sounds of my unrequited pleas.

And if no one is listening, I will talk about love to myself.

Monica Bacelli in the role of Cherubino at the Royal Opera House, London, April 1994.

0.01–0.19	0.19–0.33	0.33–0.49	0.49–1.07
Section A. The aria begins with an upbeat tone, as Cherubino shows off to Susanna. Clarinets strengthen the texture of the palpitating string accompaniment	The second part of section A. The orchestral parts remain fairly constant, sustaining the gentle pattering accompaniment	A yearning tension creeps into the melody	The first part of section A is repeated
Non so più cosa son, cosa faccio, or di foco, ora sono di ghiaccio, ogni donna cangiar di colore, ogni donna mi fa palpitar, ogni donna mi fa palpitar, ogni donna mi fa palpitar.	Solo ai nomi d'amor, di diletto, mi si turba, mi s'altera il petto e a parlare mi sforza d'amore	un desio, un desio ch'io non posso spiegar, un desio, un desio ch'io non posso spiegar!	Non so più cosa son ...

An initiation ceremony at a masonic lodge in Vienna, with Mozart seated on the far right. Painting by Ignaz Unterberter, c.1784.

Mozart the Man

Wolfgang Amadeus Mozart was a strange paradox: a sublimely gifted composer and yet a man with a most coarse and infantile sense of humour. Born the son of a violinist and composer in the Austrian town of Salzburg in 1756, he started to compose at three. By the age of twelve he had toured Europe as a performer and composed many pieces of music, including three operas. He lived at first in Salzburg, and then briefly in Paris (1777–79), but he spent most of his life in Vienna, where he came into contact with Haydn and, briefly, the young Beethoven. In 1782 Mozart married a singer, Constanze Weber, and two years later he joined the Freemasons. Typhus, financial worries and overwork are believed to have hastened his early death and pauper's burial at the age of thirty-five in 1791. The legend that he was murdered by rival composer Antonio Salieri has no basis in truth.

1.07–1.28	1.28–1.41	1.41–2.01
Section B. Notice how the voice stays more or less on one note while the violins take on a more yearning tone, almost as if they were panting	The second part of section B	Return to the first part of section B, but to a slightly different melody
Parlo d'amor vegliando, parlo d'amor	che il suon dei vani	Parlo d'amor vegliando, parlo
sognando, all'acqua, all'ombre, ai	accenti portano via	d'amor sognando, all'acqua,
monti, ai fiori, all'erbe, ai fonti, all'eco,	con sé, portano via	all'ombre, ai monti, ai fiori, all'erbe,
all'aria, ai venti,	con sé.	ai fonti, all'eco, all'aria, ai venti,

Mozart the Composer

Despite being universally hailed as one of the greatest composers that ever lived, following his death Mozart was not nearly as influential as he was popular. Perhaps his music is too self-contained: all his pieces are perfectly formed constructions in themselves, and it is hard to imagine how other composers could either imitate or develop new musical ideas from them. His music has been variously described as divine, pure, elegant, perfect and sublime. His works can be emotionally enigmatic, relying for their effect on beauty of form and sureness of touch more than on clearly defined emotional states. Even so, there is a dark, brooding character to some of his music that occasionally betrays the turbulence beneath the surface of its elegant appearance. The G minor symphony, *Don Giovanni* and the opening of his *Requiem* contain examples of this darker side, and rank among his finest works.

MASTERWORKS

Orchestral
1778	Sinfonia Concertante
1786	Piano Concerto in A major
1786	Horn Concerto in E flat major
1786	Piano Concerto in C major
1787	Eine Kleine Nachtmusik – Serenade for Strings
1788	Symphony No. 40 in G minor
1788	Symphony No. 41 in C major, "Jupiter"
1791	Clarinet Concerto

Chamber
1787	Quintet for Strings in G minor
1789	Clarinet Quintet

Opera and choral
1783	Mass in C minor
1787	Don Giovanni
1789	Così fan Tutte
1791	Die Zauberflöte (The Magic Flute)
1791	Requiem in D minor

2.01

Exact repetition of the second part of section B

2.19–2.35

The mood turns very quiet, with chords on the strings punctuating Cherubino's words

2.35–2.44

The music is very reflective here, as if Cherubino were talking to himself

2.44–2.49

The aria ends boldly, with a slight note of defiance

che il suon dei vani accenti portano via con sé,

portano via con sé

E se non ho chi m'oda, e se non ho

chi m'oda,

parlo d'amor con

me, con me,

par
d'amo

con me

BEETHOVEN'S PATHÉTIQUE SONATA

Finale: Rondo

An utterly untamed personality.
Johann Wolfgang von Goethe, describing Beethoven in 1812

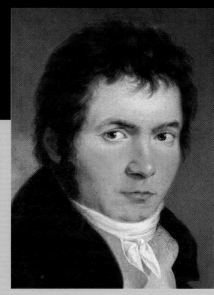

Portrait of Ludwig van Beethoven painted in 1804 by J.W. Mahler.

Beethoven himself labelled this sonata "Pathétique," not, as was often the case with descriptive titles, the publisher. The title clearly refers to the music's turbulent moods of pathos and suffering. From the opening moments of the first movement, thundering minor chords alternate with dramatic downward runs. After a short, singing adagio, the finale returns to something of the first movement's revolutionary temperament. It is in a minor key and, reflecting Beethoven's own nature, is punctuated by sudden loud bursts of passion alternating with a gentler, more lyrical strain of music. As a typical last-movement rondo of the Classical period, the main theme occurs four times with new material sandwiched between each hearing. The form might have been standard, but to those who heard the "Pathétique" sonata when it was first performed in 1798, the intensity of its expression was entirely new.

Beethoven the Man

Prince, what you are, you are by accident of birth; what I am, I am of myself. There are and there will be thousands of princes but there will only ever be one Beethoven.

Beethoven, in a letter to Prince Lichnowsky, 1806

Ludwig van Beethoven was born in Bonn in 1770, in an age of revolution. In his early childhood, America won freedom from the British in the War of Independence, and not long afterward the repercussions of the French Revolution were to affect the whole of Europe. Beethoven was himself a revolutionary, not just in the way he thought about music but in his rebellious character as well. He fought against his father's rigorous musical training and refused to don airs and graces for the aristocrats (such as Prince Lichnowsky, to whom the "Pathétique" was dedicated) who paid him his living.

From 1796, when Beethoven was still in his twenties, he began to lose his hearing and as a consequence became increasingly isolated from friends and society. Often frantically in love but never having the love that he so desired returned to him, Beethoven was a lonely, depressed and often desperate man. His tempestuous will and revolutionary zeal never left him, however, and it was these positive qualities that kept him going through his bleakest hours. "I was on the point of putting an end to my life," he wrote in 1802, "the only thing that held me back was my art. For indeed it seemed impossible to leave this world before I had produced all the works which I felt the urge to compose."

He lived alone all his life but for a brief and bitter episode as guardian to his orphaned nephew, Karl. By the time of his death in

Beethoven's ear trumpet lying on the manuscript of his Third Symphony, "Eroica."

0.01–0.20	0.20–0.37	0.37	0.48	1.10
The main theme (theme A). Tension begins to creep in quite quickly, from 0.10	A loud, assertive chord announces the second half of the main theme	Fast triplets mark theme B	A short, quiet statement leads straight back into the fast triplets (0.58), which reach a climax at 1.05 with a loud chord and a descending scale	Theme A returns for the second time

In stark contrast to Mozart's pauper's burial, Beethoven's funeral was attended by some 10,000 people.

1827, Beethoven was widely recognized as Europe's greatest contemporary composer. Even so, his apartments, like his manuscripts, betrayed the turmoil of a man whose only means of verbal communication was through a mixture of writing and signing. His first language, however, was evidently music and not German.

Beethoven the Composer

The two sides of Beethoven's musical nature are, on the one hand, grandeur and passion, and, on the other, serenity and lyricism.

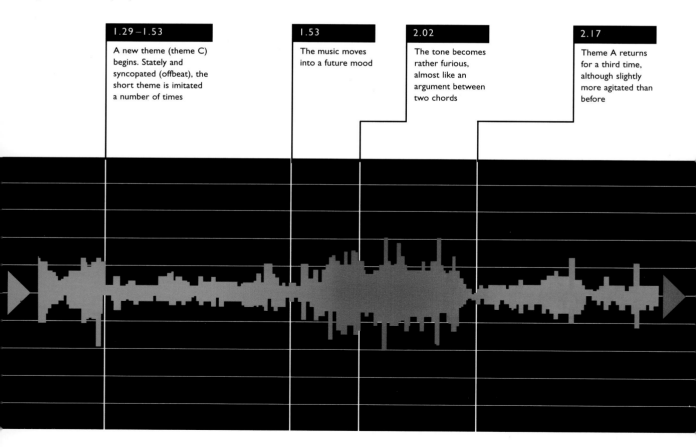

1.29 – 1.53
A new theme (theme C) begins. Stately and syncopated (offbeat), the short theme is imitated a number of times

1.53
The music moves into a future mood

2.02
The tone becomes rather furious, almost like an argument between two chords

2.17
Theme A returns for a third time, although slightly more agitated than before

These traits are apparent in equal proportion throughout his work and it is the skilful way in which his music moves from one mood to the other that defines Beethoven's distinctive musical style. His works can be roughly divided into three periods: Early (1790–1800), Middle (1800–12) and Late (1812–27). During the course of his career his music moved away from the restraint and elegance of the Classical period of Mozart and Haydn, and towards a musical language of experimental form and intense emotional expression. The string quartet, the symphony and the piano sonata are the three forms to which Beethoven contributed the most throughout his composing life, and it is by following the chronological development of these works that listeners can best understand the nature and excitement of the bold musical steps he took in his continuing search for ever profounder means of musical expression.

MASTERWORKS

Orchestral
1800	Symphony No. 1
1803	Symphony No. 3, "Eroica"
1806	Violin Concerto in D major
1808	Symphony No. 6, "Pastoral"
1809	Piano Concerto No. 5, "Emperor"
1812	Symphony No. 7
1824	Symphony No. 9, "Choral"

Choral and opera
1804–5	Fidelio (opera)
1819–23	Missa Solemnis (Mass in D)

Piano sonatas
1801	No. 14, "Moonlight"
1805	No. 23, "Appassionata"
1818	No. 29, "Hammerklavier"

Chamber
1802–3	"Kreutzer" Violin Sonata
1805–6	"Rasumovsky" String Quartets
1826	String Quartet in C sharp minor

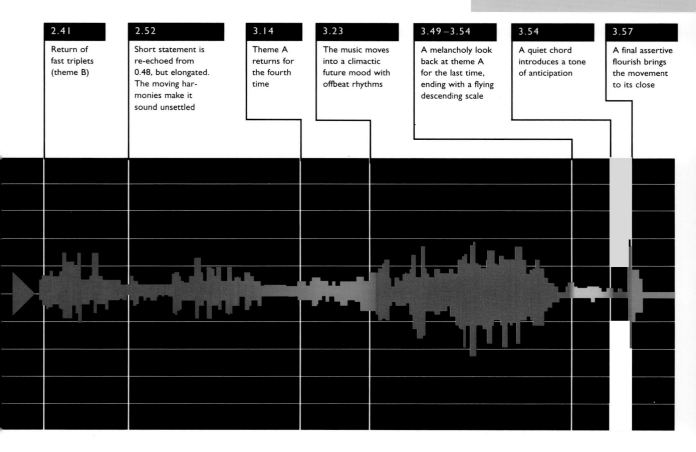

2.41
Return of fast triplets (theme B)

2.52
Short statement is re-echoed from 0.48, but elongated. The moving harmonies make it sound unsettled

3.14
Theme A returns for the fourth time

3.23
The music moves into a climactic future mood with offbeat rhythms

3.49–3.54
A melancholy look back at theme A for the last time, ending with a flying descending scale

3.54
A quiet chord introduces a tone of anticipation

3.57
A final assertive flourish brings the movement to its close

SCHUBERT'S TROUT QUINTET

Fourth Movement: Variations

Schubert put down notes where other men resort to words.
Robert Schumann, in a letter of 1829

Schubert at work on a composition.

Following the success of Schubert's song "Die Forelle" (The Trout), the composer agreed to write a set of variations on the melody at the request of an enthusiastic amateur musician and friend, Sylvester Paumgartner. He started composing the piece while he was on holiday in Upper Austria during April 1819, and the final result was his five-movement *Trout Quintet*.

The fourth movement, featured on **Track 33** of your CD, is a set of variations on the Trout song theme, and is the only movement of the quintet that relates to the song. The tune itself is played, more or less unaltered, by a different instrument in each of the first four variations, with the other instruments playing decoratively around it. In the last variation, violin and cello play alternate phrases while the piano ripples the original accompaniment from Schubert's earlier setting. In the light-hearted song text, the virtues of the trout are extolled: "Nimbler than we are for all our arms and legs. Wily as can be too. They can spell 'angler' as well as most folk. And that fellow with the rod thinks they can't see him. He's stirring the water up; but it takes more than that to beat a trout."

Schubert the Man

His character was a mixture of tenderness, coarseness, sensuality and candour, sociability and melancholy.
Johann Mayrhofer (1787–1836)

In his lifetime, Schubert was overshadowed by the reputations of Beethoven, Mozart and Haydn. Many of his songs and much of his chamber and solo piano music were never published in his day, nor were many performed in the concert halls or grand palaces of Europe.

SCORING

1 violin
1 viola
1 cello
1 double-bass
1 piano

Instead, most of his music was first played among a circle of friends with Schubert himself on the viola or at the piano.

Schubert was born in Liechtenthal, near Vienna in 1797, the son of a music teacher and a cook. After music lessons from his father he won a scholarship to the imperial court chapel, where he studied composition and theory with the famous Italian composer, Antonio Salieri. Until 1818 he taught, as assistant master, at his father's school. After that he only just managed to scrape together a living as a composer until his untimely death from syphilis in 1828. Schubert was only thirty-one when he died, at the height of his creative powers.

Schubert the Composer

Schubert had a supreme gift as a melodist. All of his tunes are easily singable, and it was accordingly for the voice that he composed his

The title page of Schubert's song "Die Forelle," from which the *Trout Quintet* took its name and inspiration.

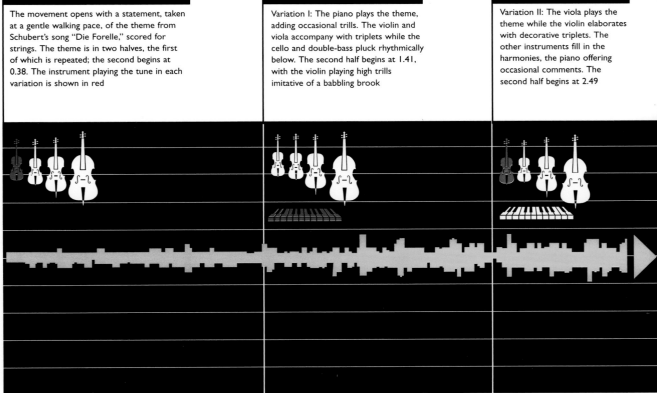

0.01–1.07

The movement opens with a statement, taken at a gentle walking pace, of the theme from Schubert's song "Die Forelle," scored for strings. The theme is in two halves, the first of which is repeated; the second begins at 0.38. The instrument playing the tune in each variation is shown in red

1.07–2.09

Variation I: The piano plays the theme, adding occasional trills. The violin and viola accompany with triplets while the cello and double-bass pluck rhythmically below. The second half begins at 1.41, with the violin playing high trills imitative of a babbling brook

2.09–3.16

Variation II: The viola plays the theme while the violin elaborates with decorative triplets. The other instruments fill in the harmonies, the piano offering occasional comments. The second half begins at 2.49

most intimate and subtly expressive music. He was never theatrical enough to succeed with opera, but as the composer of over 600 songs for voice and piano, Schubert's legacy in this aspect of vocal music is unrivalled by any other composer. The introspective character of his style and the purity of his melodies are eminently suited to the intimate media of small chamber groups or music for solo piano. Most of his greatest works were composed within the last five years of his short life.

MASTERWORKS

Song cycles
1823 Die schöne Müllerin (The Fair Maid of the Mill)
1827 Die Winterreise (The Winter's Journey)

Orchestral
1816 Symphony No. 4 in C minor, "Tragic"
1822 Symphony No. 8 in B minor, "Unfinished"
1828 Symphony No. 9 in C major, "The Great"

Piano
1822 Wanderer Fantasy
1827 8 Impromptus
1828 Sonata in B flat major

Chamber
1824 String Quartet in D Minor, "Death and the Maiden"
1824 Octet for clarinet, horn, bassoon, double-bass and string quartet
1826 String Quartet in G major
1827 Piano Trio in E flat major
1827 Piano Trio in B flat major
1828 String Quintet in C major

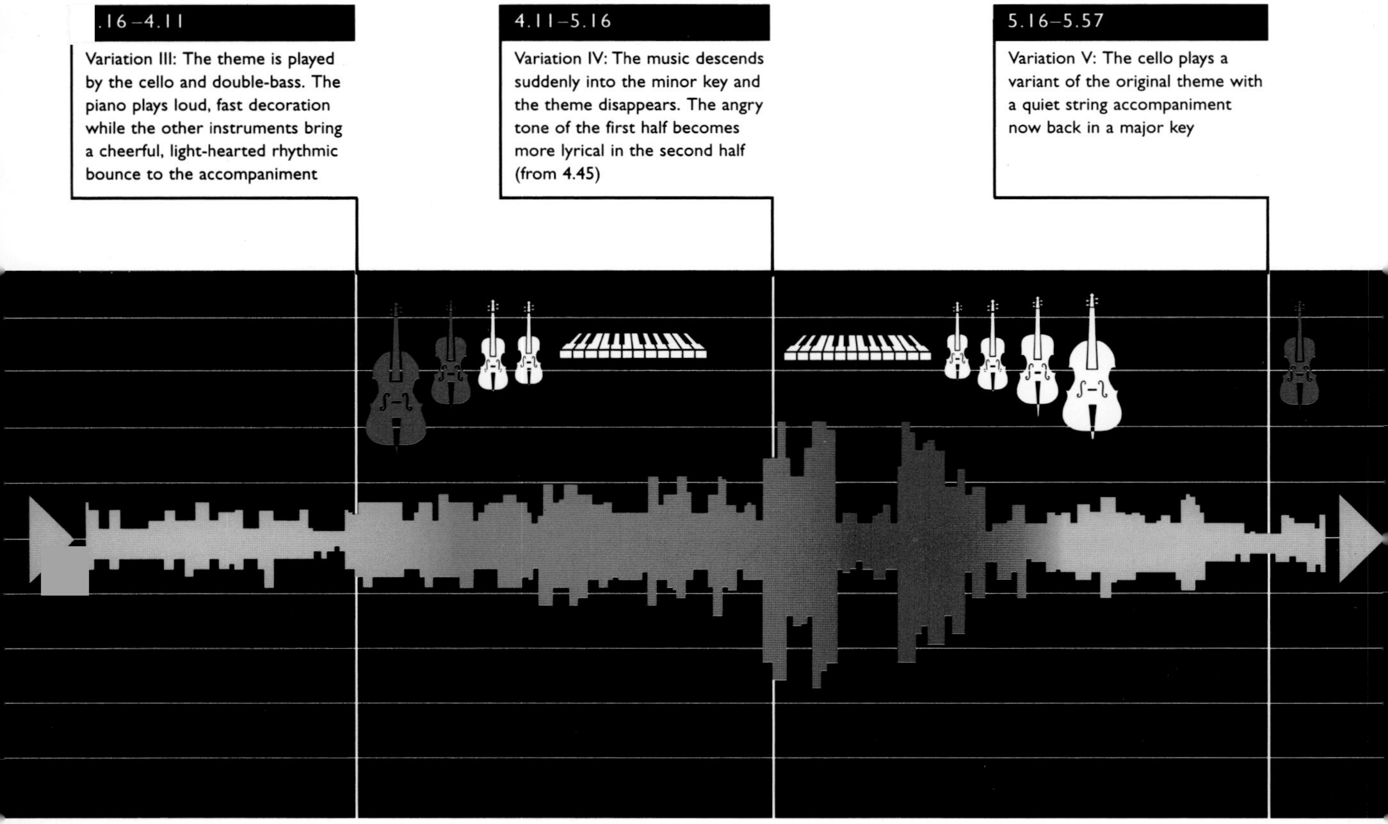

.16–4.11

Variation III: The theme is played by the cello and double-bass. The piano plays loud, fast decoration while the other instruments bring a cheerful, light-hearted rhythmic bounce to the accompaniment

4.11–5.16

Variation IV: The music descends suddenly into the minor key and the theme disappears. The angry tone of the first half becomes more lyrical in the second half (from 4.45)

5.16–5.57

Variation V: The cello plays a variant of the original theme with a quiet string accompaniment now back in a major key

A Schubert Evening at the Home of Joseph von Spaun by Moritz von Schwind, picturing Schubert at the piano.

5.57–6.45

The second half of Variation V becomes slightly more unsettled and reflective, with occasional dark shades

6.45–8.06

Final cheerful statement of the theme, back in the original key. The theme is shared by violin and cello, with the rippling triplet accompaniment of the violin and piano parts taken straight from Schubert's song. While the cello plays the tune, the violin takes on the sound of a leaping trout. The movement has a pleasant and unassuming finish

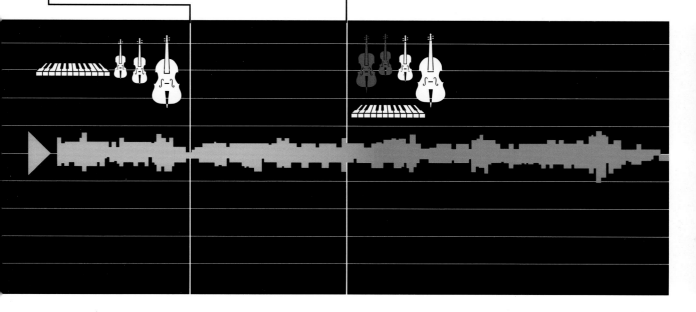

DEBUSSY'S LA MER
Second movement: "Jeux de vagues" (Play of the waves)

Monet's *Impression: Sunrise*, 1872, gave its name to the Impressionist movement.

I was destined for the wonderful life of a sailor. It was only chance that diverted me; even so I have retained a sincere passion for the sea.
Claude Debussy, in a letter of 1903

The sea was a major force of inspiration for Debussy, just as it was for Monet and other French Impressionist painters, and Debussy wrote several pieces inspired by it. *La Mer* was conceived as three symphonic seascapes in 1903. The first and last movements were originally called "Calm sea around the Iles Sanguinaires" and "The wind makes the sea dance," but were renamed for the final version "Dawn to midday on the sea" and "Dialogue of the wind and the sea." Only the middle movement, "Jeux de vagues" or "Play of the waves," kept its title. The underlying theme of the piece, though – a whole day at sea, from dawn to stormy evening – remained unaltered.

The work was composed while Debussy was on holiday in 1905 and was inspired, in part, by the south coast of England. At its Paris premiere in October of that year, *La Mer* met with a barrage of critical disapproval. One French critic pointed out that "the audience seemed disappointed; they expected the ocean, something big, something colossal, but all they got was some agitated water in a saucer." Debussy's reputation travelled far and fast. By 1909 *La Mer* was

ORCHESTRATION

Woodwind	Percussion
3 flutes	1 kettledrum
1 piccolo	1 pair of cymbals
2 oboes	1 tam-tam (gong)
1 English horn	1 triangle
2 clarinets	1 glockenspiel
3 bassoons	
1 contrabassoon	**Strings**
	violins
Brass	violas
4 horns	cellos
3 trumpets	double-basses
2 cornets	
3 trombones	**Other**
1 tuba	2 harps

receiving its U.S. premiere in Chicago. "There is no end of queer and unusual effects in orchestration," wrote a critic in the *Chicago Tribune*, "no end of harmonic combinations and progressions that are so unusual that they sound hideously ugly."

However violently some of Debussy's contemporaries were prepared to voice their dislike for his music, the composer's reputation and international stature were impossible to dislodge. Nowadays, *La Mer* is considered a landmark in the history of orchestral music and the cornerstone of Impressionist music.

Debussy the Man

Debussy was a man of shy and awkward disposition, well mannered, humorous and quietly determined. He was born in St. Germain-en-Laye in 1862 and his father was a travelling salesman, a printer's

The original title page of Debussy's *La Mer*, based on a print by Hokusai.

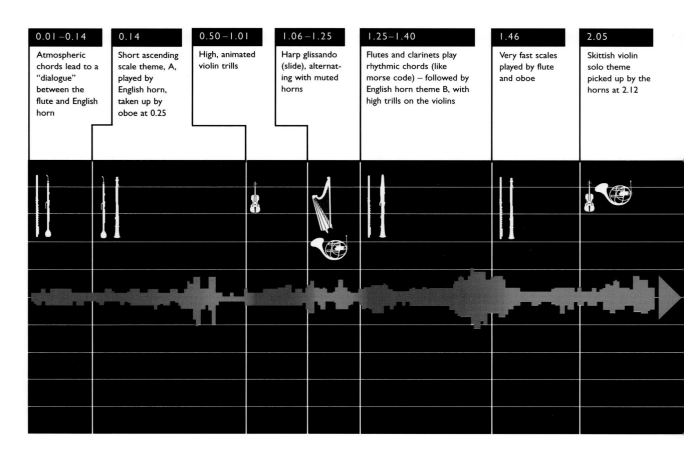

0.01–0.14	0.14	0.50–1.01	1.06–1.25	1.25–1.40	1.46	2.05
Atmospheric chords lead to a "dialogue" between the flute and English horn	Short ascending scale theme, A, played by English horn, taken up by oboe at 0.25	High, animated violin trills	Harp glissando (slide), alternating with muted horns	Flutes and clarinets play rhythmic chords (like morse code) – followed by English horn theme B, with high trills on the violins	Very fast scales played by flute and oboe	Skittish violin solo theme picked up by the horns at 2.12

Photographic portrait of
Claude Debussy.

assistant, and later an office clerk. He entered the Paris Conservatoire at the age of ten and, after years of intensive study in both piano and composition, the twenty-two-year-old Debussy won the prestigious Prix de Rome for his now neglected composition, *L'Enfant prodigue*. As his fame spread, so too did the international sphere of his influence – Stravinsky was one of many composers to admit the importance of Debussy in his work – while at the same time many critics vilified Debussy's music as modernist and insane. In 1899 Debussy married a model, Rosalie Texier, but the marriage was not a success. Five years later she attempted suicide after he left her for Emma Bardac, the wife of a wealthy banker. Later, when the scandal had died down, Debussy married Mme Bardac, who bore him a daughter, Claude-Emma or Chouchou. He died at the height of his fame from the after-effects of a colostomy operation on March 25, 1918.

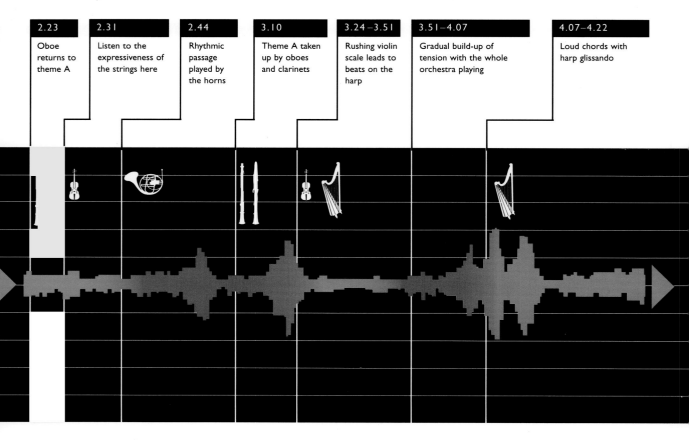

2.23	2.31	2.44	3.10	3.24–3.51	3.51–4.07	4.07–4.22
Oboe returns to theme A	Listen to the expressiveness of the strings here	Rhythmic passage played by the horns	Theme A taken up by oboes and clarinets	Rushing violin scale leads to beats on the harp	Gradual build-up of tension with the whole orchestra playing	Loud chords with harp glissando

Debussy the Composer

There is scarcely one twentieth-century composer of historical and international importance, with the notable exception of Arnold Schoenberg, who has not at some point fallen under the spell of Debussy's influence. As the father of modern music, Debussy formed new ways of looking at music, redefining the rules of harmony, melody and form. He was a sublimely talented orchestrator, and his innovations in the realm of piano music were as historically important as those of Liszt or Beethoven before him. Debussy preferred the term "Symbolist" to "Impressionist" as a description of his work; even so, his music has an extraordinary ability to evoke visual images through the subtle and sensual interplay of musical moods. This is perhaps why his music was so often associated early on in his career with the principles of Impressionism.

MASTERWORKS

Orchestral

1894	Prélude à l'après-midi d'un faune
1897–9	Nocturnes
1905–12	Images

Opera

1901	Pelléas et Mélisande

Solo piano

1888–91	Deux arabesques
1901	Suite, pour le piano
1903	Estampes
1905	Suite bergamasque
1905–8	Images
1908	Children's Corner
1910–13	Préludes
1915	Etudes (Studies)

Chamber

1893	String Quartet in G minor
1913	Syrinx, for solo flute
1915	Cello Sonata

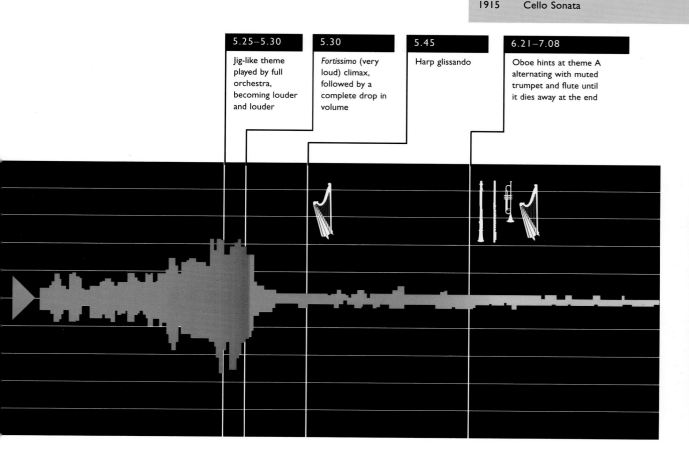

5.25–5.30
Jig-like theme played by full orchestra, becoming louder and louder

5.30
Fortissimo (very loud) climax, followed by a complete drop in volume

5.45
Harp glissando

6.21–7.08
Oboe hints at theme A alternating with muted trumpet and flute until it dies away at the end

Chapter 5
Into the Unknown:
Listening to a Piece for the First Time

It often happens that we walk into a room where an unidentified piece of music is playing, or that we hear pieces of music on the radio without catching the title of the work or the name of the composer. Only then are we completely free of preconceptions. Only by listening to a work we have never heard before, without knowing what it is or who composed it, and then slowly adding layers of background information, are we able to understand how historical context and facts about a composer's life can influence our understanding of a piece of music. This chapter looks at the way our preconceptions affect our reactions to music, and examines the challenges of listening to unfamiliar music.

It is difficult to overestimate the degree to which we are all influenced by our preconceptions, but preconceptions are not necessarily a bad thing in music, because they can help to provide abstract music with a meaning. It is known, for example, that the French Romantic composer, Hector Berlioz, died a lonely man after a life of shattered illusions. We know too that Berlioz, in later life, allowed his hair to grow in a wild style, demonstrating his complete non-interest in personal vanity and worldly affairs, as though his mind were always on a higher plane. Anyone who has even once set eyes on a portrait of Berlioz will remember his aquiline features, his fiery eyes and concentrated, withering glare. How can we possibly ignore this image once we have seen it? The face of the man and knowledge of his turbulently romantic life are almost impossible to separate from his music.

In reality, though, we are influenced by more than just a few scanty details about a composer's history. The media are responsible for shaping our views on so many matters, it is hardly surprising that they have a huge impact on our interpretation of music as well. For instance, how many romantic love films have we seen in which the culminating kiss is accompanied by a loud, slow, climactic tune played by violins with full orchestral backing? Has the film industry led us to believe that this type of music is always synonymous with romantic love, just as other styles have become associated with car chases, alien beasts or Wild Western shoot-outs? Any of these Hollywood styles of music might display a passing resemblance to any passage from Beethoven or Tchaikovsky, so the films themselves have now come to influence, however subliminally, our understanding of the classics.

Less subliminal, though, are the effects of relistening to classics that have been used as background music for films. Take David Lean's poignant 1945 film, *Brief Encounter*. How many people can listen to Rachmaninov's Second Piano Concerto without thinking of the secret

Celia Johnson and Trevor Howard in *Brief Encounter*. Rachmaninov's heart-rending Piano Concerto No. 2 was an inspired choice as the music for the soundtrack.

lovers (Celia Johnson and Trevor Howard) running to meet one another in the steamy half-dark of a suburban railway station? Similarly, Mozart's Piano Concerto No. 21 in C major became inextricably linked in the popular imagination to the Swedish film *Elvira Madigan* when record companies began to market records of the music as "Mozart's Elvira Madigan Concerto." Anyone who has seen Stanley Kubrick's cult film, *A Clockwork Orange*, is unlikely to hear Beethoven's Ninth Symphony without disturbing images of violence springing to mind, while Richard Strauss's tone poem for orchestra, *Also sprach Zarathustra*, conjures up images of outer space for those who have seen the science-fiction fantasy, *2001: A Space Odyssey*.

The environment in which we hear a piece of music can also affect the way we perceive it. A beautiful church with fine ecclesiastical acoustics and rays of coloured light streaming through a stained glass window can make even the dullest organ fugue sound magnificent, whereas the same piece on the car radio in a traffic jam might bore us rigid. But what happens when we listen to music we know nothing about, and about which we have only the smallest armoury of pre-conceived understanding?

The music on **Tracks 35–38** has been specially chosen because it is unlikely to be recognized. First, run through the checklist below of some of the best ways of listening to classical music. Then, with these in mind, listen to the short piece on **Track 35**.

A CHECKLIST FOR LISTENING

• Try to follow the musical mood of the music. What kind of mood does the music start with: PAST, PRESENT or FUTURE? How often does the mood change, and what is happening in the music to make it change?

• Does the music suggest a specific historical period or country?

• Are there any recognizable refrains or melodies that keep returning?

• What sort of visual images, if any, does the music conjure up?

• Which adjectives best describe the overall character of the piece?

• Does it help to tap out the beat?

Finally, try to imagine how the musicians and conductor would look if you were watching the piece being performed in a concert hall. If you get lost or wonder where the music is heading, try if possible to sing along, because this is a good way of finding your bearings.

A still from the controversial film, *A Clockwork Orange*, in which Beethoven's Ninth Symphony was used to sinister effect.

Beautiful surroundings can make us much more receptive to the beauty of music.

These ideas should give you a feel for the general shape and expressive message of the piece after just one hearing. You might also find it helpful to synchronize your breathing to the ebb and flow of the sound. Try imagining the music as a giant air bag that swells as it gets louder, faster and more intense, and releases itself as the activity and commotion subside. By breathing with the music (something that many performers do instinctively) you can transfer at least some of the responsibility for listening from the mind to the body.

Now that you have listened to **Track 35** a couple of times and have enjoyed it on its own merits, you are probably anxious to discover what the piece actually is. The music in question is a musical oddity by Dvořák, the first piece from his suite of five Bagatelles for two violins, cello and harmonium. All five were composed in twelve days at the beginning of May 1878. The harmonium, a small foot-pump organ, is hardly ever used by serious composers, but Dvořák incorporated it because there happened to be such an instrument in the home of his friend, Joseph Debrnov, an enthusiastic amateur musician with whom he frequently played string quartets. The fact that there is no viola part in the Bagatelles seems to imply that Dvořák (normally the viola player of the quartet) would have played the harmonium part himself.

The harmonium was originally created for the small rural church or chapel, but Dvořák's Bagatelle is scarcely religious in tone ("bagatelle" literally means a trifle or a game). The final few seconds might have a hymn-like ring to them, and perhaps there are traces of reverence in the sustained chords at the beginning of the piece, but to all intents and purposes the harmonium here comes across as a rustic instrument, not a religious one. With such a persuasively melancholic folk-style melody floating over the top of it, Dvořák brings the harmonium down to the level of the street balladeer's accordion or the

The Belle of the Village Is Asked for a Dance by Janos Janko. A rural scene from eastern Europe.

old-fashioned organ-grinder selling the latest popular songs. It is in this spirit that Dvořák's Bagatelles should be enjoyed. The mood of the first Bagatelle is predominantly PAST. The main recurring tune is in a minor key and emanates feelings of warm nostalgia and rustic charm.

On to **Track 36** where awaits a minute-long piece of piano pyrotechnics. Here, again, it is worth running through the checklist on p. 97. Singing along with the work is clearly out of the question; not even a trained opera singer could be expected to do that. Beating time is pretty difficult too. What about the mood of the music, though? Is it in PAST, PRESENT OR FUTURE? In fact, does it change at all? An instant reaction to the sheer speed and exuberance of the piece would be to think of it in a FUTURE mood. But does it really look forward? Does it really give a feeling of hurtling toward some future goal, or is it resting proudly on its own laurels?

For many people, this would be music of the PRESENT mood from start to finish. The first of Liszt's twelve Transcendental Studies, it is simply marked "Preludio." It is a sort of fanfare for piano, commanding the audience to silence as the concert begins, while at the same time providing a useful warm-up exercise for the pianist. It is, like many other examples of passages in the PRESENT, music that exists more on a functional than an emotional plane. In larger-scale works, music of the PRESENT is frequently used just to link passages of PAST and FUTURE. Second-rate performances can often be identified because they ignore this point and attach great emotional importance to every moment of functional PRESENT mood music. It is exactly the same as a speaker who obscures his meaning by accenting the least important words of a sentence.

In music, as in speech, whole phrases and sentences can be of passing functional importance only, and it is as vital for the listener to bear this in mind as it is for the performer. There is absolutely no point in frantically searching for an emotional message if the composer did not intend there to be one. In the case of Liszt's "Preludio," the whole piece serves a purely functional purpose. Four-movement works by Beethoven, Mozart and Haydn frequently featured a whole movement in the PRESENT, often an elegant minuet or another dance form, to provide breathing space between two movements of a more intense, expressive nature.

The spidery figure of Franz Liszt at the piano, in a caricature by J.P. Dantan.

The music on **Track 37** is of an altogether different mould. This uncomplicated piece, less than two minutes long, might seem on the face of it just too simple to qualify for any scrutiny at all – but what is it supposed to be about? After running through the checklist on p. 97, listen to the track once again, this time examining the three pictures opposite, and try to decide which of the images is most appropriate to the style and mood of the music.

By the end of the piece you will probably have decided that picture **c** visually best describes the music you have just heard. But how did you come to this conclusion before you knew anything about the background and history of the piece? The truth is that all of us have come to associate certain musical sounds with visual images. For example, brass band marches make us think of soldiers and Strauss waltzes of Viennese ballroom dancers. So what of the music on **Track 37**? The mood is predominantly PAST in atmosphere, though some may feel a slight ambiguity between the PAST and PRESENT here. No one would go so far as to describe this music as cheerful or dynamic, though, which explains why you were less likely to have chosen the bright still life in picture **a** or the lively dancer in picture **b**.

The music is a funeral march composed by Henry Purcell in London in 1695. The English diarist John Evelyn described this period as "an extraordinarily sickly time especially of the smallpox, of which divers considerable persons died." One victim of smallpox was thirty-two-year-old Queen Mary II of England, a much-loved monarch whose death in December 1694 was mourned by all levels of society. Purcell's March was played with solemn dignity at the funeral service in London's Westminster Abbey on March 5, 1695. The March consists of five simple phrases, all with the same long–short–short–long metre (all five are repeated), and is scored for four Flatt Trumpets, instruments more resembling trombones than trumpets, with a slide that moves backward and forward behind the player's shoulder.

Looking at visual images while listening is perhaps one of the best ways to effect a subliminal concentration and helps you use your preconceptions to apply meaning to music. Even if you chose an image that turned out to have no literal connection with the style or mood of the music, it is of no importance. There is no right or wrong about your reactions to a piece: music is too subjective for absolutes.

Chalk drawing of Henry Purcell by Godfrey Kneller, c.1690.

a. *Still Life with a Melon*, Pierre Auguste Renoir, c.1890.

b. *The Dancer Maud Allan*, Otto Marcus, 1906.

c. *Burial at Ornans*, Gustave Courbet, 1850.

The meaning of vocal music is often conveyed by the facial expressions and strident gestures of the performer. Here Claire Powell plays Hermia in Benjamin Britten's opera *A Midsummer Night's Dream*.

Finally on to **Track 38**. The music instantly conveys tension and panic: the piece is unequivocally FUTURE in mood. The singing is in Italian. Is it possible to enjoy music without being able to understand the words that are being sung? The answer, of course, is yes, although it goes without saying that an understanding of the words will improve your understanding of a song and increase the pleasure you derive from it. Without a knowledge of Italian it is only possible to appreciate the music on **Track 38** on a limited level. Because the music in question was taken from an opera, you can assume that it was intended to be staged with costumes and sets appropriate to the drama in question. You can also surmise that the characters here would be posturing in such a way as to make their message visually as well as vocally accessible. You might also guess that the dramatic action takes place somewhere in the middle of the opera and that you have therefore missed out on all the build-up of plot and characters that would usually contribute to your musical understanding of what is going on. How, in these circumstances, are you supposed to enjoy this music at all?

The solution is simply by association with something else. For example, the great Act III aria from Puccini's last opera, *Turandot*, became a world-wide hit for Luciano Pavarotti when it was used as the TV theme tune to the Football World Cup in 1990. But how many people who bought and enjoyed that CD actually knew what "Nessun Dorma" meant? "No man shall sleep…But my secret lies hidden within me, no one shall discover my name." What do these words have to do with football? Why will no man sleep and why is a person's name such a secret? The answers to these questions didn't seem to matter to most of those who bought the CD. For them the music was a reminder of the thrill of World Cup football, of the sight of their heroes battering balls into goals and of the hundreds of thousands of spectators roaring and cheering; as such, the music lifted and inspired them each time they heard it. The visual images of the sport replaced those other things (plot, character, drama, and so on) that contribute to make "Nessun Dorma" such a thrilling aria in its proper context. But who is to say who has really enjoyed "Nessun Dorma" most, the football fan or the opera buff? It is impossible to compare enjoyment levels in this way.

With **Track 38** all you really have to do is to experience the general air of dramatic panic, a FUTURE mood in music and a breathless foreign discussion. Not an ideal situation, but you can still enjoy the sound, the noise that everyone is making, the unsettling effect of those sudden accents in the orchestra, and pick up some feeling for the atmosphere of the drama from the urgent tone of voice of the singers and their breathless dialogue.

In reality this short recitative comes from Verdi's opera, *Il trovatore* (The Troubadour), written in 1853. The hero and heroine's touching but risky rendezvous is interrupted by a messenger with the news that the hero's supposed mother has been captured and is being prepared for burning at the stake. Our hero gasps in horror; his beloved notices him trembling; he orders men to rescue his mother.

A portrait of Giuseppe Verdi at about the time he composed *Il trovatore*.

Knowing what is actually happening probably improves listening considerably. As a general rule, where vocal music is concerned, it is always best to find a translation of the words. The alternative is to use your imagination to give the music whatever meaning seems most appropriate. If none of this seems to work, never despair. The system is now in place to listen to any music, famous or obscure, and to listen to it in such a way as to allow the subconscious mind to concentrate attentively while the conscious mind is occupied with images; PAST, PRESENT and FUTURE moods; and the other approaches to listening discussed in the checklist on p. 97. Listening to classical music need never be a self-conscious exercise. It takes only a wide-open mind for the eager listener to soon learn to appreciate it.

Chapter 6
Musical Journeys:
What to Listen to Next

You've fallen for a wonderful piece of music and would love to know how to find something similar but have no idea where to start looking for it. This is a common problem. In reality, no two pieces are exactly the same. Perhaps the surest way is to start by looking for pieces by the same composer, written at about the same time in his or her career. Even then, it is surprising just how different such works can be. The passion and drive of Beethoven's Fifth Symphony, for example, assumes a completely different manner from the pastoral serenities of his Sixth, yet both works are of more or less equal length, were composed for orchestras of the same size, and at the same time of his life.

Each of the following musical journeys takes as its starting point one of the seven masterpieces from Chapter 4, and pursues the particular musical style or theme of that piece through five other works as recommendations for future listening. It is worth bearing in mind that all the pieces on Tracks 28–34 (with the exception of Tchaikovsky's *1812 Overture* and possibly Tallis's *Audivi vocem*) are sections or movements of longer works, and it is worth listening to these pieces in their proper context before forging off in new directions.

JOURNEY 1: Russian Nationalism

A Religious Procession in the Province of Kursk, painting by Ilya Repin, 1880–83.

Point of Departure:
Tchaikovsky's 1812 Overture
(CD Track 28)

First and foremost I am a Russian.
Tchaikovsky, in a letter to Mme von
Meck, 1888

The Napoleonic Wars triggered a wave of Russian patriotism at the start of the nineteenth century, and music soon began to reflect nationalist preoccupations. Glinka started the Russian nationalist tradition in music with his operas *Russlan and Ludmilla* and *The Life of the Tsar*, and the seminal fantasy on two Russian themes, *Kamarinskaya*. Other composers soon followed suit. They incorporated whole folksongs into their works, the style and lilt of which influenced the composition of new melodies as well as the folk-inspired harmonies and rhythms. The nationalist movement in music lasted right up to the death of Shostokovich in 1975, and even a short list of its leading figures testifies to the strength and artistic importance of this movement: Borodin, Cui, Tchaikovsky, Balakirev, Mussorgsky, Rimsky-Korsakov, Glazunov, Stravinsky, Prokofiev, Rachmaninov and Shostokovich were among the nationalists, some of whose works are recommended below.

1. Alexander Borodin Polovtsian Dances

These famous dances show Borodin composing in an overtly Russian folk style. They come from his epic, sprawling opera, *Prince Igor*, in which the hero escapes the prison of Khan Kontchak, leaving behind his son Vladimir, who has fallen in love with Kontchak's daughter. Borodin died before he was able to complete the opera, which was eventually finished by his compatriots Glazunov and Rimsky-Korsakov. It is rarely performed outside Russia.

2. Modest Mussorgsky St. John's Night on a Bare Mountain

More eccentric in style than Borodin, Mussorgsky nonetheless imbued everything he composed with a distinctly Russian flavour. *St. John's Night on a Bare Mountain*, composed in 1867, was originally a thirteen-minute, single movement for large orchestra, but the composer later incorporated it into his unfinished opera, *Sorochinsky Fair*. Mussorgsky is best known for his opera *Boris Godunov* (based on a story by Pushkin) and the piano suite *Pictures at an Exhibition*, later orchestrated by Ravel.

3. Mily Balakirev Piano Sonata

Mily Balakirev was a late-flowering Romantic and one of the famous group of five Russian nationalist composers known as "the Kutchka" or "the Mighty Handful" (the others being Cui, Mussorgsky, Borodin and Rimsky-Korsakov). This piano sonata of 1905 starts with a flowing melody for the right hand alone and is a perfect example of the way a folksong can be transformed into a musical work of art.

4. Nikolai Rimsky-Korsakov Russian Easter Festival Overture

Russian composers have long been obsessed with colourful and exotic orchestration, and none more so than Rimsky-Korsakov. Conjuring images of Russian religious festivities, *The Russian Easter Festival Overture* was an innovative work that managed to create a new sound from a conventional orchestra and a few well-known liturgical themes.

5. Igor Stravinsky The Rite of Spring

Stravinsky's ritualistic ballet, *The Rite of Spring*, caused a riot when it was premiered in Paris in 1913. But the vociferous anti-modernists who shouted it down should have noticed how much of this work had its roots in the soil of the Russian nationalist tradition. Stravinsky, after all, was a pupil of Rimsky-Korsakov, and this early work is partly inspired by his master's style.

The Russian composers Glazunov and Rimsky-Korsakov.

JOURNEY 2: Music of the Church

Point of Departure: Tallis's Audivi vocem (CD Track 29)

When it happens that I am moved more by the music than the words which it accompanies, I confess I am guilty of a grave sin.
St. Augustine, *Confessions, c.* AD 600

Several features of religious music have remained more or less unchanged for as long as composers have been writing for the church. One such element is the hypnotic, static or rapt mood of church music – the same quality of stillness that has recently become so popular in the works of modern composers like the Estonian Arvo Pärt, the English composer John Tavener, and the Pole Henryk Górecki (sometimes known as "Holy Minimalists"). Another element common to most religious music is restraint; works such as Tallis's *Audivi vocem* tend not to wander too far from the tone established at the outset. Sudden changes in volume or texture were very uncommon in church music before the eighteenth century and, of course, with music whose function is to induce prayer and religious reverence, the tone is always serious and profound.

1. Gregorian chant

Medieval Gregorian chant is perhaps associated more than any other religious music with the church; it is certainly the most suitable music for the echoing acoustics of a large medieval cathedral or abbey. Named after Pope Gregory I, Gregorian chant is characterized by musical objectivity and other-worldliness – qualities that have made it exceptionally popular in recent years.

2. Johann Sebastian Bach St. Matthew Passion

For many, Bach's three-hour setting of the Passion According to St. Matthew is the supreme work of Christian music. Bach had set out to create a monument of musical religious devotion, and he succeeded in producing a religious masterpiece of epic proportions. With a narrator

A concert at the time of Bach. The conductor stands behind the organist.

singing the story and soloists playing the parts of Christ, Pilate, Peter and other characters, the *St. Matthew Passion* is closer to opera than any other work of his exhaustive output.

3. **George Frideric Handel** Messiah

Handel's religious music is more human and less spiritual than that of Bach or Tallis. The *Messiah* (1742) is Handel's most popular oratorio, and his robust, persuasive style illuminates passages of the Bible with the supreme consistency of indisputable genius.

4. **Franz Joseph Haydn** The Creation

Haydn's oratorio *The Creation* (1795) opens with a representation of chaos and then goes on to portray the creation of heaven and earth, the appearance of life on earth and finally the creation of Adam and Eve. Handel's influence on Haydn is particularly evident in *The Creation*, with its English text, musical depictions of nature and vivid characterizations. The strange and unsettled harmonies of the opening foreshadow music of the Romantic age.

A late fifteenth-century painting of Mary Queen of Heaven, surrounded by angels playing musical instruments.

5. **Ludwig van Beethoven** Missa Solemnis

The Mass in D, known as the *Missa Solemnis*, was considered by Beethoven to be his greatest work. Like his teacher Haydn, Beethoven was inspired in his later years by the music of Handel, to whom he paid tribute in the "Dona nobis pacem" section of the Mass with a quotation from the *Messiah*. The *Missa Solemnis*, which has been described as "a symphony in five movements," is certainly more passionate in mood than one might expect from a setting of the Latin Mass.

JOURNEY 3: High Baroque

Point of Departure: Vivaldi's The Four Seasons (CD Track 30)

There exists a common fallacy that all music of the first half of the eighteenth century not written by Bach was written by Handel.
Percy M. Young, *Handel*, 1947

The word "baroque" did not originally have a very positive connotation: it was used to mean "irregularly shaped," "grotesque," or "odd" (perhaps from the Spanish word *berruga*, meaning a wart). Whatever its origins, today the word is used to define a florid period of European art. In music, the period spanned from the early 1600s (the time of Monteverdi) to the mid-1800s with the richer, more decorative styles of Handel, Bach, Scarlatti and Vivaldi. This later period, ending with the death of Handel in 1759, is known as the High Baroque. High Baroque music is perhaps the easiest of all musical styles to enjoy: its harmonies are never obscure, its rhythms have a strong beat, and its melodies are easy to sing. Even though its orchestras and harmonies were not so developed as those of the Classical or Romantic eras, Baroque music is nevertheless capable of expressing the same levels of emotional power and dramatic intensity as any later style in music. The following journey follows the path of some of the most emotive works of this extraordinary period of musical history.

A lavish musical celebration in Rome to mark the birth in 1729 of the Dauphin in France.

1. Johann Sebastian Bach Concerto for Two Violins

Bach openly admired Vivaldi's concertos, many of which he arranged for different instruments. In his own concertos, Bach attached less importance to the display of virtuoso technique than did Vivaldi and other Italian composers, concentrating more on purely musical considerations. The famous concerto in D minor for two violins is one of Bach's most perfect creations.

2. Jean-Philippe Rameau Les Cyclopes

Rameau was the leading figure of the French High Baroque. His style is witty and fanciful, often displaying inspired flights of imagination. *Les Cyclopes*, a harpsichord piece written in 1724, is an extraordinary musical portrait of the one-eyed giants from Homer's *Odyssey*.

3. George Frideric Handel Music for the Royal Fireworks

Music for royal or special occasions formed an important part of Handel's output. The *Music for the Royal Fireworks*, composed for loud wind instruments to accompany out-door celebrations in 1749, was popular at the time and has remained so ever since (see p. 38).

4. Georg Philipp Telemann Table Music

Telemann was a friend of Bach's and one of the most pro-lific composers in the history of music. Sadly, he is now overshadowed by the giant reputations of Bach, Handel and Vivaldi, but his music contains moments of inspiration equal to theirs. His *Table Music* of 1733 was – as its name implies – intended as light background entertainment for banquets, and was composed for various chamber ensembles.

Gottfried Reiche, senior musician and solo trumpeter in Bach's orchestra.

5. Domenico Scarlatti Sonata in G major

Like Bach and Handel, Domenico Scarlatti was also born in 1685. He was the son of the celebrated Italian composer Alessandro Scarlatti and achieved fame for his extraordinary one-movement harpsichord sonatas – he composed more than 550 of them. He produced much of his best music in Spain, where he lived from 1728 to 1757. His music, often fiery and unpredictable, is always strangely compelling.

JOURNEY 4: Italian Opera

Point of Departure: Mozart's The Marriage of Figaro
(CD Track 31)

Opera: An exotic and irrational entertainment.
Samuel Johnson, *Dictionary*, 1755

It was fashionable during the eighteenth century for composers, of whatever nationality, to write their operas in Italian, probably because the most skilful and popular singers at the time were Italian. Handel, Gluck and Haydn all used Italian librettos, as did Mozart, but Mozart was one of the last non-Italian composers to do so (and even he used German librettos for some of his operas). With the age of Beethoven and the coming of the Romantic era, Italian operas became increasingly rare outside Italy. The leading figures of Italian opera during the early nineteenth century were Rossini, Donizetti, Bellini and Verdi. The genre culminated in the *verismo*, or realist, school in which intense tragedies, often involving poor, low-life characters, were accompanied by highly charged, emotional music. The chief *verismo* composer was Giacomo Puccini. Pietro Mascagni, Ruggiero Leoncavallo and Umberto Giordano kept the embers of this movement glowing until the death of Giordano in 1948, which effectively brought to a close the long and illustrious tradition of Italian opera.

1. Gioacchino Rossini The Barber of Seville

Featuring the same characters as those in Mozart's *The Marriage of Figaro* (both operas were based on stories by Beaumarchais), Rossini's opera is even more light-hearted than Mozart's. Rossini had a genius for combining memorable melodies with virtuoso vocal lines and orchestration; his ebullient style was better suited to comedy than tragedy.

2. Gaetano Donizetti Lucia di Lammermoor

Donizetti composed several successful comic operas, but his greatest works are his romantically inspired tragedies. *Lucia di Lammermoor*, his most popular work and one of his most intense tragedies, is full of bold

Gioacchino Rossini was during his lifetime the most successful and popular composer of operas in Italy.

melody and unashamedly passionate emotion. In *Lucia*, the heroine goes mad and stabs herself as a result of unfounded fears that her sweetheart, Edgar, has betrayed her.

3. Vincenzo Bellini I Puritani

Bellini's music is just as committed and vibrant as Donizetti's, but set on an even bigger scale. *I Puritani* was the last opera he wrote before his early death, at the age of thirty-three, in 1835. The opera's heroine Elvira, like Lucia, loses her reason because she believes her lover has been unfaithful; she refrains from committing suicide, however, and the story ends happily. The opera features many good examples of *coloratura* (florid, virtuoso singing for soprano).

4. Giuseppe Verdi Otello

Verdi's operas explore the very depths of human emotion. Hugely famous in his own lifetime (and something of a national hero at the time of Italian unification in 1871), Verdi is today considered by many to be the most important figure of Italian opera. *Otello*, his last tragedy (1887) and his most concise work, brilliantly manipulates the music to offer new insights into Shakespeare's immortal characters Othello, Desdemona and Iago. Otello is an exhausting and difficult part for the tenor to sing. Both Luciano Pavarotti and Placido Domingo have made successful modern recordings of the role.

5. Giacomo Puccini Madame Butterfly

Puccini, like so many Italian opera composers, specialized in depicting female grief. The three operas that brought him international fame and fortune (*La Bohème*, *Madame Butterfly* and *Tosca*) all involve the death of their heroines. In *Madame Butterfly*, the heroine, a young Japanese geisha girl, is led to commit suicide when her husband, an American naval officer, returns after a three-year absence accompanied by an American wife. Puccini's dramatic writing for the soprano voice is particularly fine in this opera.

Vincenzo Bellini was at the forefront of Italian Romanticism.

Frontispiece to the score for *Madame Butterfly*, 1904.

JOURNEY 5: Solo Piano

A Song Without Words, painting by
George Hamilton Barrable, 1880.

Point of Departure: Beethoven's Pathétique
Sonata (CD Track 32)

*The piano is the social instrument par excellence. It is drawing
room furniture, a sign of bourgeois prosperity, the most massive
of devices by which the young are tortured in the name of
education and the grown-up in the name of entertainment.*
Jacques Barzun, preface to *Men, Women and Pianos* by
Loesser, 1954

Beethoven started the age of piano virtuosity. His music
for the instrument reached new emotional depths and
demanded more stamina and skill from the performer
than ever before. As a result, piano manufacturers were
under constant pressure during his lifetime to develop
instruments that could take the strain of the new,
heavier style of playing and respond to the power of
sound and the range of expressive demands that
Beethoven's compositions imposed. The later pianos
used by Beethoven and his contemporaries marked the
beginning of a new age in piano-making. This led
eventually to the hugely powerful, concert-grand
Steinway sound that we are used to hearing in modern
concerts today. Mozart also composed a large corpus of beautiful piano
music, but the instrument of his day worked by a different
mechanism and achieved its own level of perfection in the 1790s. Just
as composers like Wagner and Verdi specialized in opera, so there were
many who specialized in composing music for the piano. The best-
known of these were Chopin, Schumann, Alkan, Liszt, Scriabin,
Debussy and Rachmaninov, all of whom were excellent virtuoso
players themselves. Each helped, in his own way, to broaden the instrument's artistic parameters with music that was passionate, expansive and
extremely difficult to play.

1. Robert Schumann Arabeske

Schumann composed most of his piano music for his pupil – and, later, wife – Clara Wieck. She was one of the most famous pianists of the nineteenth century and her keyboard skills far outstripped those of Schumann. This lovely, hypnotic Arabeske is one of Schumann's most measured and reflective works for piano.

2. Frederic Chopin Barcarolle (opus 60)

Like Schumann, Chopin preferred to write music on a small scale, and he devoted nearly all his efforts to an extensive corpus of miniature pieces for solo piano. This Barcarolle, or Venetian boating song, which lasts for seven or eight minutes, is longer than most. It demonstrates the advanced level of nineteenth-century virtuoso piano technique as well as Chopin's subtle shadings of musical mood.

3. Franz Liszt Les Années de pèlerinage (Years of Pilgrimage)

Franz Liszt was a true romantic in every sense, whose contributions to the development of virtuoso technique inspired manufacturers to make louder, more robust instruments toward the end of the nineteenth century. Much of Liszt's piano music is flamboyant and showy, but the three volumes of *Les Années de pèlerinage* reveal that there was also a reflective side to Liszt's musical personality.

4. Sergei Rachmaninov Etudes-tableaux

Stretching the virtuoso to even greater limits of technical endurance, Rachmaninov (who, like Liszt, had enormous hands) was also a performer-composer who wrote the largest proportion of his music for piano. His doom-laden *Etudes-tableaux* require unprecedented strength and stamina from the performer, who is required to play hundreds of notes a minute.

5. Alexander Scriabin Ninth Sonata

The Russian composer Alexander Scriabin shared piano classes with Rachmaninov in 1884. But while Rachmaninov's compositions were notably conservative in style, Scriabin's were arrestingly modern. The Ninth Sonata, nicknamed "Black Mass," represents the summation of his preoccupation with religious mysticism.

Portrait of Franz Liszt, the most influential nineteenth-century composer of piano music. He was followed by an adoring public at all his concerts.

115

JOURNEY 6: Viennese Chamber Music

View of Vienna by Bernardo Bellotto, 1759–61.

Point of Departure:
Schubert's Trout Quintet
(CD Track 33)

Classicism is health, romanticism is sickness.
Johann Wolfgang von Goethe,
Conversations with Eckermann, 1827

At the end of the eighteenth and beginning of the nineteenth centuries Vienna was so full of musical talent that it became known as the music capital of Europe. Haydn, Mozart, Beethoven and Schubert were the pillars of Viennese Classicism and each composer, in his own way, demonstrated a unique affinity for chamber music forms. Haydn and Beethoven in particular emphasized the value of the string quartet as a vehicle for expressing music's profoundest thoughts. Toward the end of his life, Schubert, whose deepest musical expressions were perhaps most readily reserved for song, also produced a series of magnificent master-pieces for chamber ensembles. The C major String Quintet or the last three Quartets are examples of Schubert at his most elevated and highly charged. The ten best-known String Quartets of Mozart have never quite achieved the same level of popularity as his music in other forms. They are difficult to perform successfully in concert despite having all the usual hallmarks of the composer's genius. The six String Quintets (for a string quartet plus an extra viola) are easier to listen to and represent the pinnacle of Mozart's forays into chamber music.

1. Franz Joseph Haydn Seven Last Words

The *Seven Last Words* was one of Haydn's personal favourites. A musical representation of Christ's seven last words on the cross, it is in seven slow movements and ends with a terrifying depiction of an earthquake ("Il terremoto"). The work was originally conceived for orchestra, but Haydn later arranged it for string quartet as well as a cantata with solo singers; the quartet version is arguably the best. It is the most spiritual and hypnotic of all Haydn's chamber works.

2. Wolfgang Amadeus Mozart Clarinet Quintet in A major
Although the clarinet was a recent invention in Mozart's time, the composer wrote a number of works for the instrument, including a beautiful trio for clarinet, viola and piano; a clarinet concerto; and this quintet (for string quartet and clarinet). Written in 1789, it is the purest and most exquisite of Mozart's compositions for the instrument.

3. Franz Schubert String Quintet in C major
Schubert's C major quintet, for string quartet with an extra cello, shows a marked development from the buoyant spirits of his *Trout Quintet*, composed only nine years earlier. Schubert's melodic and harmonic invention is here at its most profound. This beautiful work was composed in the last few months of Schubert's life.

4. Johann Hummel Piano Quintet
Although Hummel was not Austrian by birth, he was a regular figure on the musical scene in Vienna at about the same time as Haydn, Beethoven and Schubert. He is best known today for his delightful trumpet concerto, but his piano quintet is equally attractive and a good example of the style of chamber music that was popular in Vienna at this time.

A chamber concert given in 1769.

5. Ludwig van Beethoven String Quartet in C sharp minor (opus 131)
Some people consider Beethoven's last quartets to be the apotheosis not only of Viennese chamber music but of all western classical music. Of course this a subjective judgment, yet no one can deny the monumental stature of these works. Opus 131 was Beethoven's favourite quartet.

JOURNEY 7: Impressionism

Point of Departure: Debussy's La Mer (CD Track 34)

It's lucky I've managed to write music because I know perfectly well I should never have been able to do anything else.
Maurice Ravel, 1904

The Ballet from "Robert le Diable" by the Impressionist painter Edgar Degas, 1876. This painting of the ballet scene from Meyerbeer's opera was commissioned by the singer Jean-Baptiste Faure.

The term "Impressionism" refers in music to works that evoke rich visual images using subtle and distinct changes in mood. The term is most often applied to the French composers Debussy, Ravel and Satie, and even though Debussy disliked the term, he has always been considered the leading figure of the Impressionist movement. The style of music was not exclusively French, however: similar characteristics appear in the late piano music of Brahms and Liszt, in passages from Wagner's operas, the songs of Hugo Wolf and the symphonies of Ralph Vaughan Williams.

I. Erik Satie Gnossienne No. I

The music of Erik Satie is so distilled and individual that the roots of his musical language and the sources of his inspiration remain something of a mystery. Satie was very eccentric, but despite his complicated personality he managed to achieve a unique level of musical simplicity in his *Gnossiennes* for solo piano, which were inspired by pictures on an ancient Greek vase of women from Knossos. His famous piano pieces, *Gymnopédies*, were also inspired by the purity of Greek art.

2. Maurice Ravel Une barque sur l'océan (A small boat on the ocean)
Ravel's dazzling depiction of a small, storm–tossed boat on the ocean was a milestone of pianistic Impressionism when it appeared in 1904. Here the listener can easily identify the ebbing and flowing of a swirling sea. "Une barque sur l'océan" is the third part of Ravel's five-movement masterpiece, *Miroirs* (Mirrors). In 1906 he orchestrated the movement, which is sometimes played as a separate concert piece.

3. Claude Debussy Estampes (Engravings)
We have already heard how Debussy was able to conjure images of the sea in *La Mer*, but no understanding of Impressionism in music could be complete without an understanding of his piano pieces. *Estampes*, of 1903, is one his most evocative works. The three movements are entitled "Pagodes" (Pagodas), "Soirée dans Grenade" (Evening in Granada) and "Jardins sous la pluie" (Gardens in the Rain).

Maurice Ravel, Debussy's greatest rival, here pictured at the piano.

4. Ralph Vaughan Williams A London Symphony
Ralph Vaughan Williams's suggestive and colourful orchestration was learned from Maurice Ravel, from whom he took lessons in 1908. His Second Symphony of 1914 evokes the atmosphere of London both at its quiet dawn and during the City's bustling business hours. It includes echoes of chiming church bells as well as Cockney street cries. *A London Symphony* cemented Vaughan Williams's reputation as a major new talent and brought, for the first time, the influences of French Impressionism to a new school of British composers.

5. Olivier Messiaen Turangalila
Messiaen was the last of the great French Impressionist composers. In *Turangalila*, a monumental symphony composed in 1948, Messiaen explores themes of life and love and draws on eastern as well as western musical influences. The score demands an especially large orchestra, a virtuoso solo pianist, a vastly expanded percussion section requiring seven players and a futuristic early electronic instrument known as the "ondes Martenot" (Martenot waves).

Chapter 7

A Listeners' Guide to Forty Great Composers

The good composer is slowly discovered; the bad composer is slowly found out.
Ernest Newman (1868–1959)

As the celebrated music writer Ernest Newman pointed out, it takes time to understand the different styles and idioms of each of the great composers. The problem is always where to start and, unfortunately, composers are so different from one another that no single piece of advice could possibly work for them all. Some composers wrote their greatest music toward the end of their lives, others excelled when they were young. There are those whose finest achievements were written for the orchestra while others specialized in works for the piano. The following guide examines forty great masters from the listener's point of view, identifying the best approach to each composer's musical style and recommending which works to listen to first.

Johann Sebastian Bach (1685–1750) Germany

Neither as dazzlingly virtuosic as Vivaldi, as humanely emotional as Handel, as surprising as Scarlatti, nor as daring as Rameau – yet many would argue that Bach is the greatest Baroque composer. There is a relaxed beauty, a rapt self-acceptance to Bach's music that puts it on a spiritually therapeutic plane far removed from the expressive effects of other musical styles. His output was consistent and his hypnotic style, based on repeated rhythms and sophisticated harmonic modulations, is suited to music of all kinds, vocal or instrumental, sacred or profane. It is best, if possible, to hear his music played on period instruments, perhaps the only exception being his harpsichord music, which many find more palatable and expressive on the piano (an instrument Bach never used). All of Bach's music is worth hearing, but a good starter's path should take in the "Brandenburg" Concertos, the *St. Matthew Passion*, the Mass in B minor, his Concerto for Two Violins, the Orchestral Suites and the "Goldberg" Variations.

Béla Bartók (1881–1945) Hungary/U.S.A.

Bartók's six String Quartets and the opera *Duke Bluebeard's Castle* are the works that earned Bartók his international reputation as one of the great "modernists" of the early twentieth century. Now, even so long after they were composed, these pieces still sound modern, dissonant and aggressively rhythmic, but the strength and individuality of their character remains as alluring as ever.

Those wanting to sample an easier side to Bartók should listen to the tuneful *Divertimento for Strings* and the *Romanian Folkdances* or, more popular still, the *Concerto for Orchestra*.

Ludwig van Beethoven (1770–1827) Germany

Beethoven's music falls into three distinct periods, conveniently labelled Early, Middle and Late. Common opinion has it that his Late period string quartets (Nos. 12–16) are his finest masterpieces and rank among the greatest works ever composed. This may well be true, but it is best to understand something about his earlier styles before listening to his later pieces. Beethoven's music hinges, almost more than any other composer's, on the crucial contrasts between music that is passionate and music that is lyrical – and some of the best pieces to demonstrate this are the "Pathétique," "Appassionata" and "Moonlight" piano sonatas; the Third, Fifth and

Seventh Symphonies; the serenely beautiful Violin Concerto; and his only opera, *Fidelio*. Most of these pieces come from his Middle period. Of the titanic works from his Late period, the "Hammerklavier" sonata (opus 106), the *Missa Solemnis* and the Ninth Symphony are less appreciably melodic and more densely expressive. These are treats to leave until last.

Hector Berlioz (1803–69) France

Berlioz was the leading figure of Romantic music during his lifetime. All his major works were composed for orchestra and – with the exception of his warm cantata, *L'Enfance du Christ,* and his ardent song cycle, *Nuits d'été* – were mostly composed for a large orchestra, which was unusual in its day. Berlioz's sophisticated genius and appealing emotional naiveté are

inseparable elements of his musical makeup. *Symphonie fantastique* – a frank portrayal of his infatuation with an Irish actress – and *Harold in Italy*, a symphony for orchestra and solo viola, are good examples of this. The huge *Requiem* has never been recorded to complete satisfaction and needs to be heard live first of all. *Romeo and Juliet*, a four-movement symphony with choral interludes, is one of his greatest works but, like his dramatic cantata, *La Damnation de Faust*, its large-scale form is hard to grasp at first, even though the stories of both are well known. His greatest masterpiece is his opera, *The Trojans*, but the full impact of this outstanding piece will be easier to appreciate once you have heard the *Symphonie fantastique* and other earlier works.

Leonard Bernstein (1918–90) U.S.A.

Leonard Bernstein was a composer who moved easily between the splashy big-band style of the American Broadway

musical and the serious spiritual world of symphonies and religious works (principally, as Bernstein himself put it, about "me down here, looking up to find Him"). Whatever his style, Bernstein tended to wear his heart on his sleeve, so none of his music is oppressively cerebral or unnecessarily complicated. Best among his serious works are the *Chichester Psalms* and his Symphony No. 2 ("The Age of Anxiety"), which are loaded with pathos and intensely felt emotion. *West Side Story*,

the Broadway musical drawn from Shakespeare's *Romeo and Juliet*, is so well known it needs no introduction.

Johannes Brahms (1833–97) Germany

There is nothing outrageous or innovative about Brahms's music. Unlike many famous composers of his time, Brahms did not experiment with rhythm, harmony, orchestration, form or anything else, yet from an early age he found his own very distinct voice. The texture of his music is consistently rich and warm, sometimes soporifically so, and the mood fluctuates between sweet nostalgia and an almost Beethovenian sense of proud defiance. Of the lighter pieces, his *Hungarian Dances* for orchestra or the enchanting *Liebeslieder Waltzes* for mixed voices and piano duet offer the best way in. For a more serious side to Brahms's musical personality, the four symphonies, the two piano concertos, his Violin Concerto and the Clarinet Quintet are all perfect examples of his deft

skill as a composer of big works. Those whose first experience of Brahms is with the broadly teutonic *German Requiem* or the evasive late piano pieces (opuses 116–19) might well wish they had started elsewhere. Do not give up, though: these works will reveal themselves in the end.

Benjamin Britten (1913–76) England

Here is a composer who is really not so easy to understand. His music needs to be approached by degrees and, sooner or later, you will begin to enjoy it. The *Variations on a Theme of Frank Bridge* for string orchestra was the piece that first established his international reputation in 1936 and, with its attractive mix of popular contrasted movements, it makes an immediate and decisive impact on the listener. But it was primarily in the field of vocal music that Britten excelled, and here the words

often help to expel any ambiguity from the music. His *Serenade for Tenor, Horn and Strings* – settings to music of famous unrelated poems – is a masterpiece by any standards; so too is the harrowing *War Requiem*, a mixture of the Latin Mass text and war poems by Wilfred Owen. For anyone wanting to enjoy Britten's music without having to try too hard, his lighter music, such as *Soirées and matinées musicales* (orchestral suites based on Rossini tunes) or the *Young Person's Guide to the Orchestra* are the most obviously safe bets; for those who still feel wary of "modern" music, the Canticles, the Cello Suites and the Third String Quartet should be saved for a later date.

Anton Bruckner (1824–96)
Austria

A love for Bruckner's music is unlikely to come immediately, and, of the great late Romantic composers, he is not the best one to try first. The problem here seems to be that the heart of his output consists of a cycle of long complicated symphonies.

Unlike Mahler, Bruckner was not a natural melodist, and where there is no strongly defined melody it is easy for listeners to lose their way. During his lifetime Bruckner was not so popular – his music was described by one critic as being "poisoned with the sulphur of Hell" – but we can now appreciate the breadth and vision of his style, those enormous climactic crescendos and his ability to sustain tension over a seemingly endless musical canvas. Try Symphony No. 1 first.

Frédéric Chopin (1810–49) Poland

Chopin is one of the least troublesome of all Romantic composers to listen to. All of his music involves piano, most of it solo. Perhaps the most charming and instantly appealing of

all his works are the Waltzes for solo piano: light, melodic and endlessly pleasing. The Nocturnes, wistful pieces of night-time music, are perhaps a little more profound than the Waltzes, though no less instant in their appeal. The short Mazurkas, inspired by Chopin's yearning for his native Poland, show one of the greatest aspects of Chopin's genius: his ability to create an atmosphere of intense intimacy in a very short space of time. Among his greatest works are the Preludes (opus 28), a set of twenty-four pieces conceived to be played as one large work; the two piano concertos, each as sensuous and tuneful as the other; his Barcarolle, an impassioned version of a Venetian boating song; and the four contrasting Ballades, of which No. 1 in G minor is famed for its glorious uplifting central melody. The noisy Polonaises are not the best starting point.

Claude Debussy (1862–1918)
France

Debussy was a supreme master of the art of orchestration, as well as the most gifted innovator of music for solo piano since Liszt, and it is therefore in these two areas that you should begin

an exploration of his music. *La Mer* has been discussed on pp. 90–3, but of equal importance are the *Nocturnes* and *Images*, also for orchestra. Those who find his music disconcertingly tuneless might seek comfort in his sublime shifts of orchestral colour and texture, and his works for solo piano can be enjoyed in the same way. In his *Estampes*, for instance, or the sensually evocative *Préludes*, Debussy manages such a wide range of beautiful sonorities that the listener hardly notices the elusive nature of his melodic lines. The secret of listening to Debussy is, first and foremost, to enjoy the sound and worry about everything else later. Leave his late pieces for last: the *Etudes*, for instance, or the Cello Sonata might not make an impact at first. Try the attractive *Arabesques* or the *Suite bergamasque* for solo piano instead.

Antonin Dvořák
(1841–1904) Bohemia

In 1877, Antonin Dvořák was described as "the most god-gifted composer of the present day." Certainly, his skilful use of melody and counterpoint are exceptional for any era, and he is one of the few composers who could write music that is unambiguously happy. The first movement of his Piano Quintet is a case in point, or the last of those melodious Bagatelles for two violins, cello and harmonium (see pp. 98–9). Many of his greatest works were composed around the time of his stay in America and demonstrate an attractive blend of Moravian and American influences. The "American" String Quartet, the String Quintet in E flat and the "New World" Symphony are all wonderful examples of this. In a purely Slavonic style, his Cello Concerto, the *Slavonic Dances* and the fairy-tale opera, *Rusalka*, all testify to his genius.

Edward Elgar (1857–1934) England

The thin crusty surface of the Englishman's heart is always melted by the sound of Elgar's music. There is something in the British character – a painful inability to confront emotion perhaps – that finds a deep resonance in Elgar's music,

which has also found admirers throughout the world. The conflicts between passion and social restraint are more marked here than in any other composer of the late Romantic period. He first came to prominence with the "Enigma" Variations for orchestra (1899), highlighted by the nobility of its central "Nimrod" variation. His *Serenade* and *Introduction and Allegro* for strings are lighter but no less moving works. The First Symphony is more easily digested than the Second, and the Cello Concerto is simpler to follow than the rhapsodic Violin Concerto. But all these works, plus his rousing Catholic oratorio, *The Dream of Gerontius*, exude an elegiac warmth.

Philip Glass (b. 1937)
U.S.A.

As the core member of the American Minimalist movement, Philip Glass has earned himself a position of historical importance as well as a popularity unparalleled for a serious living composer of the late twentieth century. His style is deliberately repetitive and harmonically static, leaving room for the listener's imagination to wander off and indulge in its own free fancies. Often it is Glass's approach to each piece and the ideas behind them that differ more than the works themselves. His music is principally mood music, and his innovative techniques have been copied by lesser composers in the spirit of New Age music, and also used in films. Best start with *Akhnaten*, a thrilling opera about an ancient Egyptian monotheist king, as Glass's atmospheric music is perfectly suited to the historical and cultural context of this piece.

Edvard Grieg (1843–1907)
Norway

Today Grieg's international reputation seems to rely, for its continued well-being, on the success of three pieces, the dazzling Piano Concerto in A minor, the poignantly lyrical *Holberg Suite* for strings and the incidental music for Ibsen's play *Peer Gynt*. These works provide the most logical way into Grieg's world of ravishing sound. But his instantly recognizable Romantic and melodic style is also worked into many other pieces, some of them rarely played. The C minor Violin Sonata, for instance, the proud Cello Sonata, the many Lyric Pieces for solo piano and the delightful songs are all pieces that should be heard.

George Frideric Handel (1685–1759) Germany/England

At various times in their lives Mozart, Haydn and Beethoven all declared Handel to be the greatest composer that ever lived.

Handel produced some of the most emotional musical expressions of the Baroque era. His music is frank and forthright, focusing on the joys and sorrows of the human condition. No one could fail to be moved by the yearning sorrow of the chorus from the oratorio *Solomon*, "Draw the tear from hopeless love," or the painfully ironic chorus from *Jephtha*, "How dark, O Lord, are Thy decrees," composed as Handel was beginning to realize the horrifying extent of his blindness; and who is not uplifted by the "Hallelujah Chorus" from the *Messiah*, the *Music for the Royal Fireworks*, the *Water Music* or the riotous opening to the choral work *Dixit Dominus*? Handel's Italian operas, which number more than forty, are an acquired taste: some listeners may find them long, boring, and ultimately unconvincing. Always try to hear Handel's music played on period instruments.

Franz Joseph Haydn (1732–1809) Austria

No one can really understand Haydn's music without getting to know his string quartets. It was in this medium that he expressed his profoundest musical sentiments. But it was not always profundity and sorrow that drove his music forward; he is one of the very few composers (Dvořák is another) whose music is capable of expressing pure happiness. In all his quartets, apart from the unusual *Seven Last Words* (see pp. 116–17), he mixes movements of poignant lyrical sadness with those that are eccentrically sparkly. Listen carefully

and there is always something unusual going on. No better place to hear that than in the famous "Surprise" Symphony No. 94 in G or the six String Quartets opus 33, which Haydn described as being composed "in a new and very different manner." For these quartets he replaced the traditional minuet movement with a scherzo or "joke" movement. Among his most immediately appealing works are the oratorio *The Creation*, the *Nelson Mass*, the two cello concertos, the "Oxford" and "London" Symphonies and String Quartets opuses 55, 64 and 76.

Leoš Janáček (1854–1928) Moravia

Janáček was a disarmingly slow starter, and most of his greatest works were composed after the age of sixty. His first successful opera, *Jenůfa*, is the painful story of a village girl who accidentally becomes pregnant. When the baby is born, her

heartless old guardian throws the infant into an icy river in order to save face with the villagers. Although *Jenůfa* is the most immediately appealing of all his operas, the *Sinfonietta* is perhaps the best introduction to Janáček's style. Composed for a gymnastics display in 1926, this work was written for an expanded orchestra, including twelve trumpets, and incorporates all the hallmarks of Janáček's Czech passion and rustic excitement. On a more intimate but no less directly communicative level, his string quartets are masterpieces not to be missed. His *Glagolitic Mass* might prove tough for starters.

Franz Liszt (1811–86)
Hungary

Not all of Liszt's music is easy on the ear. At its hardest, it can sound disjointed, slow-moving and indirect; but at its easiest it is romantic, melodic and full of hot-blooded musical passion. Bearing in mind that most of what he composed was for solo piano (well over 150 hours of it), the easiest pieces to enjoy are the shorter works with strong melodic character. Of these, the *Hungarian Rhapsodies* and *Liebestraume No. 3* are the most famous. In the former, Liszt composed pieces of dazzling brilliance based on melodies inspired by Hungarian gypsy music. The *Liebestraume No. 3* (Dream of Love) is, by contrast, a sensuous piece with a beautiful melody. Among his other masterpieces are the *Transcendental Studies* (**Tracks** 20 and 36); *Années de pèlerinage*, an expansive set of works for solo piano depicting his spiritual and geographical journeys between 1848 and 1877 (p. 115); the

Faust Symphony, based on the Faust legend with an optional finale for tenor and male voice choir; and the First and Second Piano Concertos. Of these, only the piano concertos are recommended to the listener unacquainted with Liszt's tough, often elusive style.

Gustav Mahler (1860–1911)
Austria

At the heart of Mahler's output are his nine symphonies (ten, if we count the last, which was left unorchestrated at the time of his death). These are large, complex works – not just in length and variety but in their orchestration too. His Second Symphony, written in 1895, calls on a vast orchestra including 4 flutes, 4 oboes, 5 clarinets, 3 bassoons, 1 contrabassoon, 10 French horns, 10 trumpets, 4 trombones, 1 tuba, 6 timpani drums, at least 4 harps and an organ – as well as soprano and alto soloists and chorus. Symphony No. 8, the "Symphony of a Thousand," is even bigger. This doesn't mean that his music is not capable of great tenderness and intimacy: he mixes a wide range of styles within a broad late-Romantic framework. Many may already know the Adagio from Symphony No. 5 as the theme music of Visconti's 1971 film, *Death in Venice*. Starting with the Eighth or Ninth Symphonies might put some people off for good. The titanic Fifth and the shorter and lighter Fourth, however, are both good introductions to Mahler's music.

Felix Mendelssohn (1809–47) Germany

Mendelssohn was a child prodigy, more remarkable even than Mozart. His earliest masterpiece is the great String Octet (scored for two string quartets), composed when he was only sixteen. Unlike Mozart, Mendelssohn did not necessarily improve as a composer toward the end of his life. The best works to look for are his Third and Fourth Symphonies

("Scottish" and "Italian"), his Violin Concerto, the *Hebrides Overture* and the String Quartets. Nothing by Mendelssohn is bad or even difficult to grasp for the first-time listener. Although Mendelssohn was a mainstream figure of the German Romantic tradition, his music is notably feminine and Classically restrained.

Claudio Monteverdi (1567–1643) Italy

As the towering musical genius of his age, Monteverdi is a composer whose music is definitely worth exploring. *L'Orfeo*, of 1607, is the earliest opera still in the regular repertoire of opera houses around the world. With an extraordinary mixture of rustic peasant song, passionate characterization, loftily moving airs and a

well-paced storyline, it is easily the most approachable of his secular works, while the *Vespers* of 1610 are among the finest of his works for the church. *The Coronation of Poppea* is a long opera, probably too long for anyone not used to this early Baroque style. His best music is identified by lively rhythms, memorable tunes and a quick turnover of musical ideas.

Wolfgang Amadeus Mozart (1756–91) Austria

Listening to Mozart presents no problems: his music speaks very much for itself and many agree that he is one of greatest composers of all time. Those who do find fault with Mozart, though, do so on two levels: firstly, that his genius is overrated,

to the extent that many of the works composed at the beginning of his career are really not so outstanding, and, secondly, that he rarely if ever lays bare his soul in the way that Haydn and Beethoven do. Both these statements have elements of truth to them but this does not in any way denigrate Mozart's genius; it simply means that a choosy listener will get much more out of Mozart than someone who expects everything he wrote to be divinely inspired. Some of his music for solo piano, for instance, is not

terribly interesting, nor are all of the long arias from his early operas, but at its best Mozart's music is unquestionably sublime. The later works are the most rewarding, and the best places to start sampling are among Symphonies Nos. 39–41, Piano Concertos Nos. 23–27, the Clarinet Quintet, the String Quintets, the C minor Mass, the *Requiem* and his four greatest operas, *The Marriage of Figaro*, *Così fan Tutte*, *Don Giovanni* and *The Magic Flute*.

Sergei Prokofiev (1891–1953) Russia

Prokofiev's music is not a simple affair. The "Classical" Symphony or *Peter and the Wolf* might well give the impression of a composer who is readily melodious, burning to communicate and easy to enjoy, but most of Prokofiev's music is more challenging than that. In some pieces (the Fourth Piano Sonata or the opus 54 Sonatinas, for instance), you could be forgiven for not knowing at all what is going on. His operas, especially *The Fiery Angel* and *War and Peace*, are difficult pieces to penetrate, and his piano sonatas and symphonies require more suspension of disbelief than, say, those of Beethoven or Mendelssohn. The best places to start listening are the two glowing Violin Concertos, the ballet suites for *Romeo and Juliet* and *Cinderella*, Piano Concerto No. 3 in C and the third piano sonata. For a more intimate, if sometimes frustratingly elusive, side to his art, try the twenty short piano pieces, *Visions fugitives*.

Giacomo Puccini (1858–1924) Italy

Apart from the *Messa di Gloria* (not his best work) and the elegiac movement for string quartet, *Crisantemi*, the only works by Puccini that are regularly performed are his operas. His style is emotion-

ally unambiguous: rich harmonies, glowing orchestration and long flowing tunes, often rising to great surging climaxes, are the hallmarks of his style, which was so often used to accompany tragic stories of women in love. His four most successful operas are *La Bohème*, *Tosca* and *Madame Butterfly*, composed consecutively between 1893 and 1903, and his final opera, *Turandot*, about an icy Chinese Princess, unfinished at the time of his death and generally known in a version completed by the composer Franco Alfano. *La Bohème* is his most popular opera; it is at once tragic and comic, passionate and melodious – guaranteed, in fact, to appeal to anyone with a warm and uncynical heart.

Henry Purcell (1659–95) England

To enjoy early music (and Purcell only just lived early enough to qualify as an early composer), it is important not to judge it alongside later works or to criticize it for its limitations. Music is like any language: it develops and changes with time. We wouldn't say that Shakespeare was inferior to T.S. Eliot simply because the former had a smaller vocabulary at his disposal.

Similarly, Purcell may not have had the orchestra of Berlioz or the harmonic vocabulary of Debussy at his disposal, but it was the greatest music of his time, and has the power to move us now as much as it moved his contemporaries. His short opera *Dido and Aeneas* reveals the depths of his musical feeling, so too does the *Funeral Music for Queen Mary* (**Track 37**) and any of his glorious Anthems and Odes. Leave the semi-operas for later, though.

Sergei Rachmaninov (1873–1943) Russia/U.S.A.

Rachmaninov is not a composer of many moods. His greatest works are rich and gloomy, instinctively Russian and appealingly melodic. To the sensitive soul his music can appear very depressing. The *Etudes-tableaux* for solo piano (each more bitterly sorrowful than the last),

for instance, and his magnificent Second Symphony, Second Piano Sonata and Second Piano Concerto all seem like vast extended elegies. By the end of his life, Rachmaninov's ardour had cooled. His Fourth Piano Concerto, Third Symphony and Paganini Variations are well-crafted works but not as directly emotive as the earlier pieces listed above.

Maurice Ravel (1875–1937) France

Precision and craftsmanship are at the centre of Ravel's style. Like Claude Debussy, his great rival in French Impressionism, Ravel also excelled in writing for the orchestra and solo piano. Neither of his two most famous works – the ballet *Bolero*

129

(popularized by the comedy film *10*) and the short *Pavane pour une infante défunte* – is strictly typical of the rest of his small output, although both share with other works his interest in all things Spanish. *Miroirs* and *Gaspard*, both serious large-scale

piano pieces, might prove too overwhelming for some. The charming piano duet *Ma Mère l'Oye* (Mother Goose), the String Quartet, the piano suite *Tombeau de Couperin*, and the ballet *Daphnis and Chloé* are the wonderfully colourist works to listen to first.

Gioacchino Rossini (1792–1868) Italy

Rossini is best known for the gallop from his overture to the opera, *William Tell* (used for years as the theme music to the television series, the *Lone Ranger*). Rossini concentrated mostly on opera – of which he composed nearly forty – and the overtures to some of these operas best display the essence of his musical character. The overtures to *The Barber of Seville* and the *Silken Ladder*, for instance, epitomize his spirit and lively ingenuity. So too do the sonatas for strings, the most delightful of his non-operatic works. Rossini's music is always easy to appreciate at first hearing; so much so that some may find heavy doses of it a little tedious.

Arnold Schoenberg (1874–1951) Austria/U.S.A.

The very name Schoenberg, synonymous with modern, incomprehensible music, may not appeal to the uninitiated listener, but his music is worth sampling. True, he was largely responsible for rejecting the wisdom of centuries of harmonic

tradition in favour of his own serial harmonic techniques, but at heart he was an irrepressible Romantic, and even his 1942 Piano Concerto (in which he was slave to his own cerebral harmonic rules) betrays more than a hint of his previous Romantic heritage. *Verklärte Nacht* (Transfigured Night), a string sextet later reworked for string orchestra, follows the form of an eponymous poem by Richard Dehmel. It is a beautiful work of tortured psychological German expressionism, and the string orchestra version is easily the best of Schoenberg's works to start with. Another piece to try is the Chamber Symphony No. 1, a shorter work than *Verklärte Nacht*, but of a similar style. *Pierrot lunaire*, a cycle of poems (sung in a speechlike way), in short bursts might interest the beginner, but *Erwartung*, a formless monologue about a mad woman lost in a wood, is definitely one to avoid.

Franz Schubert (1797–1828) Austria

The greatest works by this most melodic of all composers come from a concentrated stretch of extraordinary creativity in the last five years of his pitifully short life. It is best to concentrate first on his

solo songs and chamber music, as Schubert particularly excelled at these musical forms. *Die schöne Müllerin* (The Fair Maid of the Mill) is melodically the most attractive of his song cycles. *Winterreise* (A Winter's Journey) is bleaker and more unusual; it was not greeted with unanimous praise by those who first heard it, but it has been recognized ever since as a supremely atmospheric masterpiece. His greatest chamber music includes the two Piano Trios, each as inspired as the other, the three last String Quartets, the F minor Fantasy for piano (four hands) and the magnificent Quintet in C major. The "Unfinished" symphony is justly famous, but the defiant spirit of its first movement is almost more typical of Beethoven than Schubert. In general, Schubert's symphonies are lighter and less argumentative than Beethoven's, but the "Great" C major symphony (No. 9) has something of Beethoven's epic grandeur, even if it lacks the older master's symphonic urgency.

Robert Schumann (1810–56)
Germany

Small-scale intimacy is Robert Schumann's strongest point. His four symphonies and one piano concerto are exceptional works of restrained Romanticism, but it is in the solo piano pieces and solo songs that his music finds its profoundest voice. Many of these works were inspired by his love for Clara Wieck, whom he married in 1840. There is no better way to get to know Schumann's music than by listening to *Dichterliebe* (A Poet's Love) – a most tender and appealing work. His early piano piece, *Papillons* opus 2, is of a similar mood and, like so many of his large-scale piano works, consists of a set of beautifully polished, subtly related miniatures. Among his most approachable works for piano are *Carnaval*, *Kinderszenen*, *Kreisleriana* and *Blumenstuck*. The *Etudes symphoniques* and *Humoreske* (also for solo piano) are harder to grasp.

Alexander Scriabin (1872–1915) Russia

Famous in his time as a leading figure of the avant-garde, Scriabin is more often associated today with the complicated piano music of his last years (Sonatas 6–10) than with the rich, passionately Russian melodic style of his youth. The Preludes opuses 11, 15, 17 and Etudes opus 8, all for solo piano, are the easiest and most enchanting of his works. Of the later pieces,

piano sonatas 5, 9 and 10 are elusive modernist pieces, frighteningly intense but short enough never to lose the listener's concentration. Avoid the symphonies at first. Of his orchestral works, begin with his *Poem of Ecstasy*: a wild, post-Romantic 25-minute piece that

is just as ecstatic and poetic as its title suggests.

Dmitri Shostakovich (1906–75) Russia

Bound by the restrictive censorship of Stalinist Russia, Shostakovich was ordered to compose in a style that would readily communicate itself to the people. In other words, he was not permitted to follow the modernist musical trends of the west, or even his own fancies if they were to lead him too far down the path of dissonance or melodic obscurity. Generally speaking, Shostakovich obliged the authorities, and his music is consequently more melodic and less dissonant than that of other composers of the time. The sixteen symphonies form the heart of his output, of which numbers Five and Seven ("Leningrad") are among the most approachable. The Tenth Symphony is an unquestionably strong work too, though some may find its predominantly gloomy tone a little claustrophobic. Otherwise the Third and Eighth String Quartets, the Second Piano Concerto and the Cello Sonata are

particularly fine works. There is also a lighter side to his music, which can be found in an ebullient group of works whose purpose was sheer entertainment. The Jazz Suites and Ballet Suites fall into this category, as do the First Piano Concerto and the rarely heard musical comedy, *Cheryomushki*.

Jean Sibelius (1865–1957)
Finland

There is a vastness in Sibelius's music, and a bleakness too. He was a large, moody Finn, a heavy drinker, a lazy worker and prone to bouts of deep depression. Most important of all his output is the cycle of seven symphonies, of which Nos. 2, 3 and 5 are the most accessible, while No. 4 is distinctly the gruffest and most ambiguous. For those who have not heard any of Sibelius's music before, the best entree is via the Violin Concerto, a work of deeply felt Northern Romanticism, or the shorter pieces for orchestra such as *Finlandia*, a seminal work of Finnish musical nationalism; the hauntingly still *Swan of Tuonela*; and *Valse triste*, the most popular of his works during his lifetime. The sensual and yet elemental music from the *Karelia Suite* is also popular with modern audiences. Sibelius's music often takes its time; the listener needs to wait for it to unwind and explain itself, but patience is well rewarded.

Richard Strauss
(1864–1949) Germany

Richard Strauss might now be regarded as one of the very last of the German Romantic composers, but in his early days he was considered a radical of the avant-garde. His operas, such as *Salome* and

Elektra, provoked violently hostile reactions in their time, and even now the rich sonorities, swirling orchestral climaxes and high-voltage emotions can easily alienate listeners of a more reserved nature. His most popular work is the waltzy Viennese opera, *Der Rosenkavalier,* but at three-and-a-half hours long, it might be better to sample his style elsewhere first. Those who like rich food and hot rooms might enjoy the *Four Last Songs* or the indulgent elegy *Metamorphosen* for twenty-three solo strings. His youthful orchestral tone-poems *Don Juan* and *Also sprach Zarathustra* are also wonderful pieces to know.

Igor Stravinsky (1882–1971)
Russia/France/U.S.A.

Stravinsky composed music in three distinct styles during his long life and it is the last (and least melodic) of these that has proved less popular with concert audiences around the world. Common to all three styles, though, is an almost Debussyan emphasis on sound, and many would argue that it is the beauty, precision and purity of sound rather than the force of the emotion that makes Stravinsky's music so enjoyable. The early period is characterized by the three ballets *The Firebird*, *Petrushka* and *The Rite of Spring*. These exciting, colourful works are full of muscle and action, and make more of an immediate impact than almost anything else he composed. In his second, neo-Classical, period (*c.*1922–55), he looks back to the elegance and form of previous centuries with his *Symphony of Psalms*, his ballet *Pulcinella* and his only full-length opera, *The Rake's Progress*.

Pyotr Tchaikovsky (1840–93) Russia

There is a case for regarding every great work of Tchaikovsky as being tinged with desperate, tragic angst. Certainly the composer himself had a miserable life and although there is a fine line in Tchaikovsky's music between tragic poignancy and sweet sentimentality, the listener is strongly advised not to discount his work as mere sentiment. The Fifth and Sixth Symphonies are unquestionably tragic; there is a haunting feel

of Russian melancholy to the arch of his tunes both here and in the lighter works as well. The three ballets, *Cinderella*, *Sleeping Beauty* and *The Nutcracker* give a rounded picture of Tchaikovsky's style in an easily accessible form. Piano Concerto No. 1 and the Violin Concerto are extremely popular, while the operas *Eugene Onegin* and *The Queen of Spades* introduce an added dimension of vivid dramatic characterization. Stick at first to his orchestral music. His chamber music is not so instantly rewarding.

Richard Wagner (1813–83) Germany

Wagner is not an easy composer to get to know. All of his important works are long German operas, but once you have acquired a taste for one, there will probably be no looking back. To get an idea of his composing style, it is best to start with a few overtures and orchestral interludes. The overture to *Tannhäuser*, so adored by the French poet Baudelaire, is a good example of Wagner's rich orchestration and seamless flow of ideas; the overture to *Die Meistersinger* is unusually tuneful, while his long winding preludes to *Lohengrin* and *Parsifal* give a flavour of the expansive timelessness of his vast operas. *Das Rheingold*, the first of the *Ring* operas, is probably the best complete work to start with – it is the shortest and has the most action-packed story. Wagner is not a composer to pick up and put down arbitrarily: his music needs effort, commitment and, above all, time from the listener; it will never please the fickle-hearted.

Giuseppe Verdi (1813–1901) Italy

The best way to get to know any of Verdi's compositions properly is to spend at least a couple of hours on them because, with the exception of the *Requiem* and a String Quartet in E minor, all of Verdi's best-known pieces are long operas. Of course there are good recordings of choruses, arias, overtures and highlights, but it is only after listening to a complete opera that you can begin to understand what this composer is trying to do. *Rigoletto* and *La Traviata* are the best operas to listen to first: each has a convincing story and features one stirring and memorable tune after another. The great operas of his late years, *Otello* and *Falstaff*, are remarkable for their incisive characterizations and total rejection of all but the most essential dramatic elements. Without the same plethora of tunes, though, these works are not so easy to assimilate on first hearing for anyone unfamiliar with Verdi's style.

Antonio Vivaldi (1678–1741) Italy

There is no composer whose music is so straightforward as Vivaldi's, and there are no great difficulties in listening to any of it. Vivaldi's style is clear, simple and melodic. Despite the frequent criticism that his music is overly repetitive – that each piece sounds very like another – listen carefully and the subtle differences in melody, texture and atmosphere, such as are demonstrated in his best-known masterpiece *The Four Seasons*, become immediately apparent. Those wishing to hear more in a similar vein to *The Four Seasons* need look no further than *L'Estro armonico* or *La Stravaganza* (each consisting of twelve violin concertos). Otherwise the choral work, *Gloria*, is a pleasant work.

GLOSSARY OF MUSICAL TERMS

Words in CAPITAL LETTERS refer to principal cross-references

a cappella (Italian, "in chapel style") Unaccompanied church choral music

absolute music Abstract music with no relation or reference to stories, paintings or other non-musical topics

accent A stress on a particular beat

accompaniment Subordinate music to the principal instrument or MELODY (usually piano)

acoustics The science of sound; the sound properties of a concert hall or room

adagio (Italian) Slow; slow movement

agitato (Italian) Restless, agitated

air A simple tune for voice or instrument

allegretto (Italian) Light, lively

allegro (Italian) Lively and fast

alto A low female voice (contralto); also refers to any instrument in that REGISTER

andante (Italian) At a moderate speed

anthem A short vocal work for the Church of England; a national HYMN

arabesque A short decorative piece, usually for piano

aria (Italian, "song") A solo song in an OPERA or ORATORIO

arietta (Italian) A light song

arrangement A piece that has been re-scored or rearranged (often for different instruments), not usually by the original composer

atonal In no particular KEY

bagatelle A short, light piece; a trifle

ballade A short dramatic piece, usually for solo piano

bar The division of music by beats; also known as a MEASURE

barcarolle Venetian gondola song or a piece in the same swaying style, often for solo piano (Chopin, Mendelssohn, Fauré)

baritone A male voice, between TENOR and BASS

bass The lowest part of a chord; the lowest male voice

beat Metric RHYTHM

bel canto (Italian) Beautiful, sustained virtuosic singing

berceuse (French) Lullaby

bolero (Spanish) A vigorous Spanish dance

cadence Concluding HARMONIES at the end of a piece

cadenza A solo show-piece section of a CONCERTO movement, shortly before the final CADENCE

canon A work in which the MELODY is stated by two or more voices in turn; also known as a "round"

cantata A vocal, usually narrative, work for one or more voices and instruments

chamber music Music for between two and twelve solo players

chant Unaccompanied vocal music in the Christian tradition

chorale A Lutheran hymn tune

chromatic Coloured, rich; music that moves by INTERVALS of a SEMITONE, or contains many notes foreign to the main KEY

clef A symbol of notation used to determine the REGISTER of notes on a STAFF e.g. TENOR, ALTO, TREBLE and BASS

coda The final section of a piece or movement

coloratura (Italian) Florid virtuosic style of (especially Italian) operatic singing

concerto A piece for one or more solo instruments and orchestra, usually in three movements

conservatory or **conservatoire** A school or college of advanced musical study

consonance A harmonically pleasing chord; the opposite of DISSONANCE

counterpoint The simultaneous combination of two or more melodies

decrescendo or **diminuendo** (Italian) Decreasing in volume

dissonance A harmonically jarring chord; the opposite of CONSONANCE

duet A chamber work for two performers e.g. a piano duet, for two performers on one piano (four hands)

duple time Music with two beats to a BAR

dynamics Relating to volume (loud and soft)

ensemble A chamber group of mixed instruments and/or voices

étude (French, "study") A technically demanding short instrumental piece

fantasy or **fantasia** Usually a work that is free from set or established rules of form, following instead the composer's fancy. Often in one, sometimes several, movements or parts

flat Lowering in PITCH, usually by a SEMITONE. Playing or singing flat means too low, and consequently out of tune

forte (_f_), fortissimo (_ff_) (Italian) Loud, very loud

fugue A piece in which melodic lines enter one by one in imitation of one another, requiring significant skill at COUNTERPOINT

gavotte A quick dance with four beats in a BAR; a fashionable movement incorporated in the Baroque SUITE

gigue, giga or **jig** A lively dance movement of a typical Baroque SUITE

glissando (Italian, "skating") Sliding up or down a scale

grave (Italian) Slow and solemn

Gregorian chant Plainsong, unaccompanied chant

harmony The sounding of two or more notes simultaneously

homophony Music in which chords and MELODY move together; the opposite of POLYPHONY

hornpipe A lively eighteenth-century English dance, particularly popular with sailors

hymn A simple song of praise, usually Christian, sung by the congregation and mostly in two or more verses

idyll A work with peaceful or pastoral associations

imitation A technique in which one voice repeats the melodic phrases of another e.g. FUGUE, CANON, etc.

impromptu A short piece, usually for solo piano, of an improvisatory nature

improvisation A piece composed on the spot, sometimes taking the form of Variations on a Theme

intermezzo (Italian, "in the middle") A short orchestral interlude during an OPERA; a short piano piece (e.g. by Brahms)

interval The distance between two notes of different PITCH

key The tonality of a piece (either MAJOR or MINOR) relating to the polarity of particular notes within the scale e.g. C major, F minor, etc.

ländler A slow Austrian dance in WALTZ time

largo (Italian) Broad and slow

legato (Italian) Smoothly

leitmotif (German, "leading motif") A recurring THEME used to symbolize characters, objects, emotions, etc., prevalent in the OPERAS of Wagner

lento (Italian) Slowly

libretto (Italian, "booklet") The text of an OPERA or ORATORIO

lied, pl. lieder (German, "song") A German song, usually for voice and piano

madrigal A secular song from the sixteenth and seventeenth centuries, generally for several unaccompanied voices

major Relating to scales, INTERVALS, chords and KEYS; the opposite of MINOR

masque A grandiose entertainment of the English seventeenth and eighteenth centuries with instrumental and vocal music, dancing, poetry, costumes and scenery

Mass or **missa** A musical setting of the words of the Roman Catholic Mass, usually for unaccompanied voices before 1650 and for soloists, chorus and orchestra thereafter

mazurka An accented Polish dance in TRIPLE TIME particularly for piano, as popularized by Chopin, Scriabin and others

measure The division of music by beats; also known as a BAR

melody Tune or THEME

meter Time signature; regular, accented beat

mezzo (Italian) Half or medium; hence mezzo-forte (*mf*), between loud and soft; mezzo-voce, with a moderate voice; mezzo-soprano, a female voice between SOPRANO and contralto

minimalism A musical style based on the hypnotic repetition of short THEMES and phrases

minor Refers to chords, INTERVALS, scales and KEYS of a flattened nature; the opposite of MAJOR

minuet, menuet, menuetto or **minuetto** A formal dance in TRIPLE TIME; also fashionable as the third movement of many eighteenth-century works

monophony A MELODY without HARMONY or accompaniment

motet A religious choral composition, usually of the Catholic church

movement A self-contained section of a work, sometimes linked to other movements

neo-Classical Twentieth-century style based on emotional restraint, formal elegance and other attributes of the Classical period; composers included Stravinsky, Poulenc and Martinu

nocturne A short lyrical piece reflecting the calm of the night, generally for solo piano or orchestra

nonet A chamber work for nine performers

notation The system or process of writing music down

note A particular TONE or PITCH of variable length

octave An INTERVAL of eight steps (twelve SEMITONES)

octet A chamber work for eight performers

opera buffa or **opéra bouffe** A light, comic opera; operetta

opera A sung, staged drama usually for orchestra, chorus and soloists, in one or more acts

opus (Latin, "work") Opus – sometimes abbreviated as op. – numbers signify the chronological sequence of publication of a composer's output

oratorio An extended setting of a religious text, usually biblical, for soloists, chorus and orchestra (e.g. Handel's *Messiah*)

orchestration The art of composing for orchestra

ornaments Extra decorative notes e.g. trills, turns, etc.

ostinato (Italian, "obstinate") A persistently repeated musical figure or RHYTHM

overture A short orchestral work generally preceding an OPERA or ballet; from the nineteenth century onward, often a single, self-sufficient concert work for orchestra

Passion A musical setting of Christian texts relating to the Crucifixion and Resurrection

pedal point A sustained note, usually BASS, with moving HARMONIES above

perfect pitch The attribute of being able to sing or identify notes from memory

135

Glossary of Musical Terms

pesante (Italian) Heavy, ponderous

phrase A section comprising a MELODY

piacevole (Italian) Pleasantly

piano (*p*), **pianissimo** (*pp*) (Italian) Quiet, very quiet

piano quintet A work for piano and STRING QUARTET, usually in several movements

piano trio A piece for piano, violin and cello, usually in several movements

pitch The REGISTER of a note

pizzicato (Italian) The technique of plucking instead of bowing on violin, viola, cello or double-bass

polonaise A lively Polish dance, usually for solo piano (e.g. by Schubert, Chopin)

polyphony A rich style of early music in two or more moving parts

prelude An introductory, instrumental piece, often in an OPERA; also a short self-contained work for piano or, less often, orchestra

presto (Italian) Very fast

programme music Music that interprets a story, landscape, poem, painting or other non-abstract THEME

quadruple time Music with four beats to a BAR

rasch (German) Quick

recitative A style of singing in an OPERA or ORATORIO used to convey narrative and provide dramatic links between ARIAS, choruses, etc. Usually accompanied by harpsichord (secco) or orchestra (accompagnato)

refrain A recurring section of a song

register The range of an instrument or a singer's voice, e.g. TENOR, BASS, SOPRANO

Requiem Setting of the Roman Catholic Mass for the dead

rest A silent pause

rhapsody A heroic, romantic piece, usually in one movement, of no fixed form or instrumentation

rhythm The part of music that relates to note lengths

rococo An elegant musical style of the French eighteenth century; also known as *style galant*

romance A single-movement work of a lyrical nature

rondo A musical form (often used for last movements by Mozart, Haydn, etc.) in which one THEME frequently returns between passages of new material, i.e. ABACADA

rubato (Italian) Expressive, flexible RHYTHM or beat

scale A progression of sequential ascending or descending notes

scherzo (Italian, "joke") A typical TRIPLE-TIME, Classical movement, usually the third, often with a middle section known as a TRIO

score The written version of a composition, showing details of all the parts, used especially by conductors

semitone Half a TONE. The smallest INTERVAL on the piano

septet A chamber work for seven performers

sextet A chamber work for six performers

sharp Augmenting in PITCH, usually by a SEMITONE. Playing or singing sharp means too high, and consequently out of tune

sonata A piece in several movements for one or two instruments

song cycle A unified collection of songs, usually for voice and piano

soprano A high female voice; also applied to instruments e.g. soprano saxophone, etc.

staff or **stave** A set of five horizontal, parallel lines on which music is written

string quartet Any work for two violins, one viola and one cello, often in four movements

suite A piece consisting of several contrasted movements, usually in the same KEY

symphony A large-scale work for orchestra, often in four movements

syncopation An accent on the off-beat (often the second or last beat) of a BAR – a constant feature of jazz

tempo (Italian) Time, pace

tenor A high male voice; also applied to instruments e.g. tenor saxophone, etc.

theme A tune or partial tune forming a central part of any piece of music

toccata (Italian, "touched") A virtuoso show-piece usually for a solo instrument

tone An INTERVAL of two SEMITONES; quality of sound

tone poem A descriptive orchestral piece in a single movement; sometimes called a symphonic poem, symphonic ballad or symphonic fantasy

treble The highest voice of a boys' choir; also relates to music or instruments in that REGISTER

tremolo (Italian, "trembling") The fast repetition of one note on a bowed instrument to produce a shivering effect

trio Music for three voices or instruments; also the middle section of a MINUET or SCHERZO movement in TRIPLE TIME

triple time Music with three beats to a BAR e.g. a WALTZ, SCHERZO, etc.

variation A modification, development or decoration of a THEME. Often as "Theme and Variations," a form of movement

verismo (Italian, "realism") A late Romantic style of Italian opera, often about lowlife characters

vibrato (Italian, "vibrating") The technique of producing a warm sound with the voice or stringed instrument

vivace (Italian) Very lively

waltz A dance in THREE TIME, either slow or fast. Sometimes for solo piano (e.g. by Chopin) and not intended for dancing

INDEX

Index

Editor Rachel Aris
Designer Blânche-Adrienne Harper

Editorial Assistant Philippa Cooper
Picture Researcher Julia Ruxton
Indexer Juliet Bending

Publishing Director Frances Gertler
Art Director Tim Foster

CD CREDITS

1 **MOZART:** Symphony No. 40 in G minor, K. 550. First movement (extract)
ACADEMY OF ST. MARTIN-IN-THE-FIELDS conducted by
SIR NEVILLE MARRINER
℗1987 EMI Records Ltd.

2 **CHOPIN:** Waltz in E flat, op. 18 (extract)
JEAN-PHILIPPE COLLARD – piano
℗1986 EMI France

3 **CHOPIN:** Waltz in A flat, op. 42 (extract)
JEAN-PHILIPPE COLLARD – piano
℗1986 EMI France

4 **CHOPIN:** Waltz in A minor, op. 34, No. 2 (extract)
JEAN-PHILIPPE COLLARD – piano
℗1986 EMI France

5 **WAGNER:** *Tristan and Isolde*. Prelude, Act 1 (extract)
BERLIN PHILHARMONIC ORCHESTRA conducted by
HERBERT VON KARAJAN
℗1972 EMI Records Ltd.

6 **SCHUBERT:** *Winterreise*, D. 911 (wds Müller). "Gute Nacht" (extracts)
DIETRICH FISCHER-DIESKAU – baritone
GERALD MOORE – piano
℗1955 EMI Records Ltd.

7 **MOZART:** *Don Giovanni* (lib. da Ponte). Act 1 recitative, "Ma qual mai s'offre"
JOAN SUTHERLAND (Donna Anna)
PHILHARMONIA ORCHESTRA conducted by
CARLO MARIA GIULINI
℗1961 EMI Records Ltd.

8 **BEETHOVEN:** Piano Sonata No. 8 in C minor, op. 13 ("Pathétique"). First movement (extract)
WALTER GIESEKING – piano
℗1957 EMI Records Ltd.

9 **OFFENBACH:** *The Tales of Hoffmann* (lib. Barbier). Act IV, "Belle nuit, ô nuit d'amour" (Barcarolle, extract)
JESSYE NORMAN (Giulietta), ANN MURRAY (Nicklausse)
ORCHESTRA AND CHORUS OF THE NATIONAL OPERA OF
THEATRE ROYAL DE LA MONNAIE, BRUSSELS (Chorus Master:
Gunter Wagner) conducted by SYLVAIN CAMBRELING
℗1988 EMI Records Ltd.

10 **DEBUSSY:** *Rêverie* (extract)
ALDO CICCOLINI – piano
℗1992 EMI France

11 **GILBERT AND SULLIVAN:** *The Mikado*. Act 1 trio, "I am so proud"
GERAINT EVANS (Ko-Ko), IAN WALLACE (Pooh-Bah)
JOHN CAMERON (Pish-Tush)
PRO ARTE ORCHESTRA conducted by SIR MALCOLM SARGENT
℗1957 EMI Records Ltd.

12 **MENDELSSOHN:** String Quartet No. 6 in F minor, op. 80. First movement (extract)
CHERUBINI QUARTET
Christoph Poppen – first violin
Harald Schoneweg – second violin
Hariolf Schlichtig – viola
Manuel Fischer-Dieskau – cello
℗1992 EMI Electrola GmbH

13 **BRAHMS:** Symphony No. 3 in F major, op. 90. Third movement (extract)
THE LONDON PHILHARMONIC conducted by
WOLFGANG SAWALLISCH
℗1992 EMI Records Ltd.

14 **DEBUSSY:** "Clair de lune" (extract)
ALDO CICCOLINI – piano
℗1992 EMI France

15 **FAURE:** *Pavane*, op. 50 (extract)
NEW PHILHARMONIA ORCHESTRA conducted by
SIR DAVID WILLCOCKS
℗1968 EMI Records Ltd.

16 **HANDEL:** *Messiah*. Part 1, "Thus saith the Lord" (extract)
DAVID THOMAS – bass
TAVERNER PLAYERS directed by ANDREW PARROTT
℗ 1989 EMI Records Ltd.

17 **VIVALDI:** *The Four Seasons*, "Autumn." Third movement (extract)
GIULIO FRANZETTI – violin
I SOLISTI DELL'ORCHESTRA FILARMONICA DELLA SCALA
conducted by RICCARDO MUTI
℗ 1994 EMI Records Ltd.

18 **BEETHOVEN:** Symphony No. 8 in F major, op. 93. First movement (extract)
LONDON CLASSICAL PLAYERS conducted by
ROGER NORRINGTON
℗1987 EMI Records Ltd.

19 **BEETHOVEN:** Symphony No. 5 in C minor, op. 67. Third movement (extract)
LONDON CLASSICAL PLAYERS conducted by
ROGER NORRINGTON
℗1989 EMI Records Ltd.

20 **LISZT:** Transcendental Study No. 2 in A minor (extract)
VLADIMIR OVCHINIKOV – piano
℗1989 EMI Records Ltd.

21 **BEETHOVEN:** String Quartet No. 15 in A minor, op. 132. Final movement (extract)
ALBAN BERG QUARTETT
Günter Pichler – first violin

Gerhard Schulz – second violin
Thomas Kakuska – viola
Valentin Erben – cello
Ⓟ 1984 EMI Records Ltd.

22 **BEETHOVEN**: Piano Sonata No. 8 in C minor, op. 13 ("Pathétique"). Second movement (extract)
WALTER GIESEKING – piano
Ⓟ 1957 EMI Records Ltd.

23 **BEETHOVEN**: Symphony No. 1 in C major, op. 21. Fourth movement (extract)
LONDON CLASSICAL PLAYERS conducted by ROGER NORRINGTON
Ⓟ 1988 EMI Records Ltd.

24 **BEETHOVEN**: Piano Concerto No. 5 in E flat major, op. 73 ("Emperor"). Third movement (extract)
YOURI EGOROV – piano
PHILHARMONIA ORCHESTRA conducted by WOLFGANG SAWALLISCH
Ⓟ 1983 EMI Records Ltd.

25 **BEETHOVEN**: String Quartet No. 7 in F major, op. 59 No. 1 ("Rasumovsky"). First movement (extract)
ALBAN BERG QUARTETT
Günter Pichler – first violin
Gerhard Schulz – second violin
Hatto Beyerle – viola
Valentin Erben – cello
Ⓟ 1979 EMI Records Ltd.

26 **BEETHOVEN**: Piano Sonata No. 32 in C minor, op. 111. First movement (extract)
STEPHEN KOVACEVICH – piano
Ⓟ 1992 EMI Records Ltd.

27 **BEETHOVEN**: String Quartet No. 13 in B flat major, op. 130. Fifth movement ("Cavatina," extract)
ALBAN BERG QUARTETT
Günter Pichler – first violin
Gerhard Schulz – second violin
Thomas Kakuska – viola
Valentin Erben – cello
Ⓟ 1983 EMI Records Ltd.

28 **TCHAIKOVSKY**: *1812 Overture*, op. 49
THE PHILADELPHIA ORCHESTRA conducted by RICCARDO MUTI
Ⓟ 1981 EMI Records Ltd.

29 **TALLIS**: *Audivi vocem* a4
TAVERNER CONSORT AND TAVERNER CHOIR directed by ANDREW PARROTT
Ⓟ 1989 EMI Records Ltd.

30 **VIVALDI**: *The Four Seasons*, "Winter." First movement
GIULIO FRANZETTI – violin
I SOLISTI DELL'ORCHESTRA FILARMONICA DELLA SCALA conducted by RICCARDO MUTI
Ⓟ 1994 EMI Records Ltd.

31 **MOZART**: *The Marriage of Figaro* (lib. da Ponte). Act I aria, "Non so più cosa son"
FIORENZA COSSOTTO (Cherubino)
PHILHARMONIA ORCHESTRA conducted by CARLO MARIA GIULINI
Ⓟ 1961 EMI Records Ltd.

32 **BEETHOVEN**: Piano Sonata No. 8 in C minor, op. 13 ("Pathétique"). Third movement
WALTER GIESEKING – piano
Ⓟ 1957 EMI Records Ltd.

33 **SCHUBERT**: Piano Quintet in A major, D. 667 ("The Trout"). Fourth movement: Variations
HEPHZIBAH MENUHIN – piano
MEMBERS OF THE AMADEUS QUARTET
Norbert Brainin – violin
Peter Schidlof – viola
Martin Lovett – cello
with J. EDWARD MERRETT – double bass
Ⓟ 1959 EMI Records Ltd.

34 **DEBUSSY**: *La Mer*. Second movement, "Jeux de vagues"
THE PHILADELPHIA ORCHESTRA conducted by RICCARDO MUTI
Ⓟ 1994 EMI Records Ltd.

35 **DVORAK**: Bagatelle, op. 47, No. 1
DOMUS
Krysia Osostowicz – violin
Timothy Boulton – violin
Richard Lester – cello
Susan Tomes – harmonium
Ⓟ 1992 Virgin Classics Ltd.

36 **LISZT**: Transcendental Study No. 1 in C major
Vladimir Ovchinikov – piano
Ⓟ 1989 EMI Records Ltd.

37 **PURCELL**: *Funeral Music for Queen Mary*. March
TAVERNER PLAYERS directed by ANDREW PARROTT
Ⓟ 1989 EMI Records Ltd.

38 **VERDI**: *Il trovatore* (lib. Cammarano). Act III recitative, "L'onda de'suoni..."
MARIA CALLAS (Leonore)
ORCHESTRA OF LA SCALA OPERA HOUSE, MILAN conducted by HERBERT VON KARAJAN
Ⓟ 1957 EMI Italiana S.p.A.

143

ACKNOWLEDGMENTS

Abbreviations
a = above; b = below; c = centre; l = left; r = right
AKG = AKG London; BAL = The Bridgeman Art Library;
ET = E.T. Archive; Hulton = Hulton Deutsch Collection Ltd;
IGDA = Archivio I.D.G.A., Milan; MEPL = Mary Evans Picture Library;
PAL = Performing Arts Library

Jacket and p. 3 (Cello) BAL/Bonhams, London (CD) Ace 4 Antonio Canova, *The Three Graces*, Daniel McGrath/By courtesy of the Board of Trustees of the Victoria and Albert Museum 8 William Harnett, *The Old Cupboard Door*. BAL/Sheffield City Art Galleries 10–11 BAL/Museo della collegiata di sant'Andrea, Empoli 12l BAL/Musée National d'Art Moderne, Paris © DACS 1995 12r BAL/Galleria degli Uffizi, Florence 13 BAL/Bibliothèque Nationale, Paris 14 Guy Le Querrec/Magnum Photos 15 Steve Granitz/Retna 16 Clive Barda/PAL 17 Dennis Stock/Magnum Photos 18 Norbert Wu/Tony Stone Images 19 BAL/University of Liverpool Art Gallery and Collections 20 Leili Muuga, *Orchestra*, 1962. BAL/Estonian Art Musuem, Tallinn 22, 22–23 (background) Clive Barda/PAL 24l IGDA/Comune, Cremone 24r IGDA/Museo del Conservatorio di Musica L. Cherubini, Florence 25l, 25ra Sue Baker/Orbis 25rc Premier Percussion, Wigston 25rb Sue Baker/Orbis 26l Premier Percussion, Wigston 26ra Erik Bohr/AKG 26rb IGDA/Metropolitan Museum of Art, The Crosby Brown Collection of Musical Instruments, New York 27l Jonathan Fisher/PAL 27c Erik Bohr/AKG 27r Boosey and Hawkes 28l, 28r Erik Bohr/AKG 29l Yamaha Kemble 29c Erik Bohr/AKG 29r James McCormick/PAL 30a L. Steinmark/Custom Medical Stock Photo/Science Photo Library 30b Jon Burbank/Hutchison Library 31 ET/Museum der Stadt, Vienna 32 British Library, London 33a Henry Berlioz by Gustave Courbet. ET/Musée d'Orsay, Paris 33b Lebrecht Collection 34 Thyssen-Bornemisza Collection/© DACS 1995 35 Reg Wilson 36a BAL/Christie's, London 36b Catherine Ashmore/Dominic Photography 37 Ron Berg/Tony Stone Images 38 BAL/Private Collection 39 BAL/Lambeth Palace Library 40a Theodore Gericault, *Sounding the Horn before the Battle*. BAL/Christie's, London 40b AKG/Suermondt-Ludwig-Museum 41 *Ein Concert in Jahre 1846*. Lithograph of Berlioz conducting, after Cajetan. AKG 42 Clive Barda/PAL 43 Erik Satie by E. Renaudin. MEPL 44 Michelangelo, *David* (detail), 1501–4. BAL/Galleria dell'Academia, Florence 46a, 46b Clive Barda/PAL 47 Hulton 48 Majestic/Icon (courtesy Kobal) 49l Felix Mendelssohn by Albert Henry Payne after Theodor Hildebrandt. AKG 49r Bildarchiv Preussischer Kulterbesitz/Institut für Musikforschung 50a Manuscript of a Polonaise by Chopin. ET/Chopin Birthplace, Poland 50b Fotomas Index 51a From the Mannesse Codex, c.1320. AKG/Universitätsbibliothek, Heidelberg 51b BAL/Museo Correr, Venice 52a AKG/Musée des Beaux-Arts, Dijon 52b Johann Franz Greipel, *A performance of Gluck's Parnaso confuso*. Erich Lessing/AKG/Kunsthistorisches Museum, Vienna 53 BAL/Staatsbibliothek Preussischer Kulturbesitz 54 AKG/Private Collection 55, 56 Clive Barda/PAL 59 MEPL 60 Raoul Dufy, *Homage to Mozart*, c.1945. BAL/Giraudon/Musée National d'Art Moderne, Paris © DACS 1995 64 AKG/Musée Historique, Versailles 66 BAL/Private Collection 67 Lebrecht Collection 68 Manuscript of the opening bars of Tchaikovsky's *1812 Overture*. Lebrecht Collection 70 ET/Biblioteca Estense, Modena 71 Hulton 72 By kind permission of the Parish Church of St. Faith, Gaywood 73 BAL/British Library, London 74 A. Dagli Orti/IGDA/Fondazione Querini Stampalia, Venice 76l A. Portio and A. Dalla Via. A. Dagli Orti/IGDA/Museo Correr, Venice 76r Caricature of Vivaldi by Pier Leone Ghezzi, 1723. AKG 78 AKG/Mozart Museum, Salzburg 79 Reg Wilson 80 AKG/Historisches Museum der Stadt, Vienna 82 BAL/Historisches Museum der Stadt, Vienna 83 AKG/Gesellschaft der Musikfreunde, Vienna 84 A. Dagli Orti/IGDA/Beethovenhaus, Bonn 86 Hulton 87 AKG 89 BAL/Historisches Museum der Stadt, Vienna 90 BAL/Musée Marmottan, Paris 91 Bibliothèque Nationale, Paris 92 MEPL 94 Amedée Ozenfant, *Still Life with Violin*, c.1922. BAL/Giraudon/Musée National d'Art Moderne © DACS 1995 96 Kinema Collection/Cineguild/Rank 97a Warner Bros (courtesy Kobal) 97b Derek Forss 98 BAL/Magyar Nemzeti Galeria, Budapest 99 Lebrecht Collection 100 AKG/National Gallery, London 101al BAL/Private Collection AKG 101b BAL/Louvre, Paris 102 Clive Barda/PAL 103 Hulton 104 Jan Breugel, The Sense of Sound, 1617. BAL/Prado, Madrid.106 BAL/Private Collection 107 BAL/Private Collection 108 Engraving by Lipsia, 1732. ET/Gesellschaft der Musikfreunde, Vienna 109 From *Master of the St. Lucy Legend*. BAL/Kress Collection, Washington DC 110 F. de Antonis/IGDA/Louvre, Paris 111 Elias Gottlieb Haussmann, *Portrait of Gottfried Reiche*. BAL/Museum für Geschichte der Stadt, Leipzig 112 ET/Museo Bibliografico Musicale, Bologna 113a Lithograph by Millet. ET/Library of La Scala, Milan 113b BAL/Private Collection 114 BAL/John Noott Galleries, Broadway 115 Portrait of Liszt by Karl Ernest Lehmann, 1839. BAL/Giraudon/Musée Renan, Paris 116 AKG/Kunsthistorisches Museum, Vienna 117 AKG 118 BAL/By courtesy of the Board of Trustees of the Victoria and Albert Museum 119 Maurice Ravel by Ouvre. ET/Library of La Scala, Milan 120 Philip Mercier, *Portrait of George Fredric Handel*. ET/Viscount Fitzharris 122al J.S. Bach by Eichhorn. MEPL 122r W.J. Mähler, *Ludwig van Beethoven*, 1815. AKG/Gesellschaft der Musikfreunde, Vienna 123al Giancarlo Costa 123bl Henri Cartier Bresson/Magnum Photos 123r MEPL 124al Dennis de Marney/Hulton 124bl ET/Gesellschaft der Musikfreunde, Vienna 124ar Eugène Delacroix, *Frederic Chopin*, 1838. BAL/Giraudon/Louvre, Paris 124br M.A. Baschet, *Claude Debussy in Rome in 1884*. BAL/Giraudon/Château de Versailles, France © DACS 1995 125l MEPL 125ar MEPL 125br Betty Freeman/Lebrecht Collection 126al MEPL 126bl ET 126r Haydn by Guttenbrunn. ET/Private Collection 127al ET/Janáček Museum, Brno 127bl Charles Laurent Marechal, *Portrait of Franz Liszt at 29*. ET/Wagner Museum, Bayreuth 127r AKG 128al Hulton 128bl ET/Museo Correr, Venice 128ar Barbara Krafft, *Portrait of Mozart*,1819. AKG/Gesellschaft der Musikfreunde, Vienna 128br Lipnitzki/MEPL 129l Giacomo Puccini by A. Rietti. ET/Puccini House, Torre del Lago 129ar MEPL 129br MEPL 130al MEPL 130bl ET/Museo Bibliografico Musicale, Bologna 130ar Egon Schiele, *Portrait of Arnold Schoenberg*. Giancarlo Costa 130br Melegh Gabor, *Portrait of Schubert*. BAL/Magyar Nemzeti Galeria, Budapest 131l MEPL 131ar AKG 131br MEPL 132al Axel Gallen-Kallela, *Portrait of Jan Sibelius*,1894. AKG/Ateneumin Taidemuseo, Helsinki 132bl Fritz Erler, *Portrait of Richard Strauss*, 1898. BAL/Private Collection 132r Jacques-Emile Blanche, *Igor Stravinsky*. ET/Musée d'Orsay, Paris © DACS 1995 133al MEPL 133bl AKG 133ar AKG 133br A. Dagli Orti/IGDA/Museo Bibliografico Musicale, Bologna Endpapers AKG CD cover Ace

While every effort has been made to trace the present copyright holders we apologize in advance for any unintentional omission or error and will be pleased to insert the appropriate acknowledgment in any subsequent edition.

The publishers would like to thank Duncan Moore and Keith Hilton at EMI and Tony Bridge at Finesplice for their invaluable help and cooperation.